CONTENTS

"HELLO"

This book is written by over 30 arts practitioners and collectives. It's aim is to share method and contextualise an ethos and practice that we all have in common: a "DIY" ethos and practice. There is a deliberately open definition of DIY: letting the artists and their definitions 'speak for themselves'.

Performance making practices are all too easily canonised and made esoteric by academics and theorists, and whilst I want there to be a careful effort made to properly contextualise and theorise our idiosyncratic and common practices, I think the content of this book is best articulated 'from the horses mouth'. Therefore this book, and the people that speak within, and the label DIY itself is seen best as an 'Imagined Community' (Anderson), or perhaps a moment of 'Communitas' (Turner).

Some particular things this book focusses on is the demystifying of (our) making practices. To share theories, methods and methodologies that are common to DIY creative practice. Arts practitioners — sharing thoughts, ideas, ideologies, issues, tasks, recipes, instructions and/or methods to encourage others to make work and embody the ethos of DIY performance making. Critically (or 'theoretically') this book will address a wide range of perspectives on "DIY" theatre, it's family resemblances in other art forms, economically, culturally and politically, and address key dichotomies between ethos and style.

With this in mind, there's no wish to essentialise or reduce the myriad practices to a hegemonic (and misleading) label or formula. I want to celebrate the diversity and breadth of views and perspectives. 'Theories' and 'practices' are shared by artists and collectives first and foremost, but the text will also include important contributions from academics, producers and key organisations and agencies. Geared at students and young artists, but also — crudely — 'each other'. I hope this text will complement the few texts on devised and collective/collaborative performance practice (and theory), and crucially add a particular agenda: to share and promote the ethos of 'DIY' performance making through practical advice, critical dialogue and action.

The emphasis will be on how we can encourage and evolve performance making (by sharing our theories and practices) and demythologise contemporary performance making practice. To help empower more artists to engage with this way of working, and to also (tacitly) promote the politic, contexts and 'discipline' involved in working in this way. Little efforts like this to catalyse and position our community are always a good thing. And this book is an effort at that.

Beyond that, this book should be seen as a creative text. A text that provokes, prescribes, instructs, advocates, plays, advises, promotes, shares... I think you can imagine the scope here.

... Enjoy

"SHIT-Good"

and doing it myself (with a little help from my friends)

Robert Daniels (Bootworks)

"DIY" theatre and performance is commonly seen as an ethos or a style. Sometimes both. The label 'DIY' has its roots in home improvement, but is variously used to define particular countercultural communities, socio-political movements, and a creative and symbolic style. In most contexts it means - despite a fair few contradictions and inconsistencies - exactly what it describes and labels: to be independent, or at least 'self-reliant'. Literally to do it oneself. It's ethos and history reaches into many other aspects of life, culture, history and society, and in turn 'Art', music, theatre, dance and performance.

Like all labels, it can be inhibiting and negative whilst also empowering and positive. "DIY" is a fairly straightforward concept to understand overall and well documented in terms of culture, music, writing, media and the fine/visual arts, as there is a wealth of material available that explicitly use the label, and trace it's axioms through history. There's a solid historical account in Spencer's *DIY: The Rise of Lo-Fi Culture* (2008) and Biel's *Beyond the Music: How Punks are saving the World with DIY ethics, Skills & Values* (2012). Both of which position core roots of DIY "as 'a youth-centred and -directed cluster of interests and practices around green radicalism, direct action politics, [and] new musical sounds and experiences... a kind of 1990s counterculture'" (McKay,1998a, in Halfacree, 2004: 69)

It's not so well documented in terms of theatre and performance history. Not in cultural and historical contexts, or in established 'scenes' and movements therein at least. Unpicking what is a DIY 'ethos' and a DIY 'style' is less distinctive, and more problematic in theatre and performance. Heddon aligns/attributes a "DiY" label to the live and performance art scene in the 60s in it's emergence as post-Avant Garde art practices distinct from it's predecessors in Fine Arts, and infiltrating fields of Dance, Theatre and Music, through to the 90's, where it becomes "an identifiable, well-managed landscape" (2012: 23). Heddon's alignment is analogous to the way in which many scholars (and artists themselves) attribute the influence of

Live/Performance Art on contemporary (especially "post-dramatic" - Lehman et al) theatre and performance.

Some people will know the term in relation to the Punk movement, and few ideologies before it that promoted self-reliance and the democratisation of knowledge (and making 'Art'). Most artists these days will be familiar with The Live Art Development Agency's annual project "DIY", which is, "an opportunity for artists working in Live Art to conceive and run unusual training and professional development projects for other artists." (thisisliveart.co.uk)

LADA have been pivotal (alongside ArtsAdmin, New Work Network and other likeminded organisations) in the sustaining of the Live Art and its 'Theatre' antecedents, and were the first, bar Glasgow's Festival of DiY Culture perhaps (which while predominately socio-politically and music-driven, encompassed a range of 'alternative lifestyle and art practices'), to really 'coin' the term with regard to performance-making.

Beyond this, the term started to crystallise for me in 'blog' articles by Hannah Nicklin and James Stenhouse/Action Hero, who each state that DIY (Theatre making) is, "about an approach and a way of working that deliberately avoids mainstream modes of production." (hannahnicklin.com), and, "something born of a place and community, and which offers a distinct alternative to the monoculture that thrives on top-down structures, (the mainstream music industry e.g.) and 'one size fits all' models of entertainment." (ilivesweat.tumblr.com). More writing by both James and Hannah can be read in this book.

Through the 70s/80s political and cultural shift, artists and activists continued to suffer under similar oppressive state apparatus. Many artists and collectives were naturally being more 'guerrilla': radically independent and politically driven. DIY-like labels were being attached to 'home grown' politically motivated activist groups like Reclaim the Streets, the Punk phenomenon and its counterculture, and in theatre and performance the emergence of a new generation of artists - nourished by the ideologies of the 'postmodern' Dance and Theatre scenes of the 60s - with concomitant funding categories developed in response to a range of work in the landscape that was becoming too difficult to label in traditional ways.

In the present landscape, not too dissimilar from the oppressive Conservative regime of the aforementioned past, the practice of DIY can be crudely divided into three camps: those that covet and employ rudimentary ('lo-fi', 'retro', 'trailing edge') technologies, those that purposely do it 'badly' or without care for quality, and those that consider dilettantism, auto-didacticism and working with anything they have in frugal ways as a political and philosophical modus operandi. There are echoes of the kind of socio-cultural contexts that inspired artists (like Forced Entertainment, Gob Squad, and in dance: Extemporary Dance, or even DV8), as well as the problematic dichotomy that has polarised practice from philosophy in the past. History - as it does - is repeating itself.

This kind of practice is now a commonplace feature of many practice-driven performance making university degree courses, where it can be argued the critical mass for this field really comes from: Forced Entertainment from Exeter, Gob Squad from Nottingham, Stans Cafe from Lancaster, a host of young artists and collectives from Dartington, Central and Leeds in the last decade, now to what we do at Chichester. The academy is cited often in relation to the way in which live art (and to extend their remit: theatre and performance) has maintained and "indeed, grown" as a robust creative and political field. My own definition is specific to a kind of 'artisan' theatre making, and an ethos - from my HE teaching - that promotes ideas of the autodidact.

Though the notion of the artist as artisan is nothing new whatsoever. This connection between a punk ethic and contemporary performance making is well made. Though for me It's a bit idyllic. A little too neat. Though it's not without genuine significance. Bootworks at one point were

definitely of the Punk-like 'garage band' ilk: we did everything 'ourselves' and figured it out by doing it. Now we're much more reflexive and refined.

Texts by practitioners and artists that aim to instigate and empower others to make things are my favourite kind. Not so long ago such 'guides' were scarce. 'Practice' was some kind of precious thing and I guess people didn't feel like giving their secrets away. In recent years it seems artists are a little more willing to share. Book by artists and collectives are becoming more commonplace, and whilst some do little more than elaborate promotional agendas, they all contribute to a more detailed and vibrant cultural awareness of the arts.

Books I found most valuable as a student and in the early days of my career were the ones that helped me widen my method/skill base. Books like Tuffnell and Crickmay's *Body Space Image*, *The Goat Island School Book*, *The Routledge Practitioner series*, or Paris and Hill's *The Guerrillas Guide to Performance Art*. Nowadays I am still drawn to texts I can use directly in and with my own work, or perhaps just share with my students: Kleon's *How to Steal Like an Artist*, Smith's *Guerrilla Art Kit*, Wrights and Sites' *Misguide to Anywhere*, Forest Fringe's *Paper Stages* ... and so on.

Whatever they can be seen to be doing in terms of sharing practice, or making practices formulaic (which isn't always a good thing) these texts are at least points of reference and departure for artists to collectively 'thicken' the identity of their practice. Some of them transcend the arcane and archaic notion of 'Art', and are paradigm shifters inasmuch as one could consider the political act of democratising art-making a defining feature of contemporary art and - I think - DIY performance.

Another defining feature of a DIY ethos lies in the notion that 'skill' is acquirable and accessible to all. It no longer has to belong to an elite. DIY books - of any kind - are full of useful advice, applied knowledge and transferable skill. Since the all-world-almanac emerged there has been an all-too-urgent awareness in the lack of knowledge and information. Funny really considering the 'information' age we live in. Auge's supermodern 'excess of information' doesn't quite round the square peg. These days we're so

accustomed to service that we expect things to run automatically. We no longer feel the need to retain the all-very-useful information. And it's not 'out there' and besetting us. In one sense we're living in a world that has all but abandoned the importance of applied, practical knowledge. The "how too" is no longer essential knowledge: we've a man/woman/robot for that. Hence the need to archive and canonise. In another sense we have Francis Bacon's promise that "knowledge is power", and a cultural revolution underpinned by the democratisation of knowledge. We have wikileaks, Wikipedia...a World Wide Web. Hive minds. Books, and websites, that hold, transmit and disseminate the precious information. Passing out knowledge, craft and ethos.

Therefore the term DIY can be formally and informally used in myriad ways. As a description of the individual as 'independent', or a label for community of 'independents': an indie-culture'. Whilst this approach and overarching ethos is not-at-all a recent phenomenon, it is only recently that we see the label being embraced and employed in particular - creative, theoretical and political - contexts. One of the most significant aspects of a DIY ethos lies in the stripping away of the excess. "Not just in terms of social veil, but also in terms of staff, financials, and tiers of management; structural innovation." (Burian in Biel, 2012: 89). Which means, in relation to theatre and performance, being a 'creative' industry in the truest sense.

In Bootworks there is little 'specialisation'; there are designated roles, but they are fluid and cooperative. We are victims and celebrants of our own talents. I handle a lot of the 'tech', James is a wiz on Photoshop (so he does the marketing), and we made Andy manage an entire rural tour once. He's a dab hand at pressing badges and laminating acetates too. Sophia is our education coordinator, and her experiences with other companies in E&O settings mean she heads up our relationship with schools and colleges. These days we (necessarily) have Becki, our Producer, handling much of the nuts and bolts we all once (badly) managed...but there are very clear points where all of us do a bit of everything. We rarely commission external 'experts', and when we do, we do so with very clear intentions and agendas.

We do it ourselves because its the ways we learned and discovered. I wasn't taught how to 'do business' or conduct myself as an artist in 'the industry', I was taught to create, and compose, and play. To take anything and everything I could - be it media, technology, literature, ideas... - and make work. The rest was up to me. As Marshall McCluhan argues "...new technology allows (maybe even forces) old technology to be put to different, often artistic, purposes." (in Spencer, 2008: 90) and growing up (as an 'ensemble', then 'cooperative', then 'company', and now 'collective') through the 90s and 00s we've made good use of this ideology. New technologies and media has been in constantly evolving, quickly making 'old' tech cheaper, more accessible and ready-to-exploit. So we have. Not because we 'had to', but because we could.

When I was at university my lecturer would call me a magpie. He thought I was very good at stealing things. 'Shiny' things. The kind of course I studied involved a lot of practice. We sampled lots of different methods and styles. Some seemed to stick with me. Others I bastardised and appropriated to make them fit. "Making good of bad rubbish", as The Wombles say, is something we like to think we do quite often. I'm not sure I can remember a time when we did anything 'properly'. As much as we have independent views, inclinations and backgrounds, we share an indifference regarding virtuosity, skill or technique. I'd like to imagine this indifference is militant political position, but really it's a kind of agnosticism. We believe in the idea, but not the dogma. As well as this, we find the act of labelling our work usually reductive and counter to our interdisciplinary practice.

With Gob Squad there was a much more conscious act of rebellion, they renounced virtuosity "in favour of attempting to achieve a purer presence on stage. Spending time with one another. Bizarre combinations. Worn out signs and shabby equipment. Noble dilettantism as a style of representation, the staging of emptiness and so on." (Gob Squad and Quinōnes, 2005: 12) We're more like bricoleurs than dilettantes. We are not adverse to notions of skill, or virtuosity, or whatever; we definitely consider some of the things we do to be highly disciplined, and the notion of a 'purer presence' definitely appeals to our inclinations, we just don't always take ourselves, and what we do too seriously. Or rather; we will happily engage with any practice we can to make work. In this sense we broaden McCluhan's ideas on the appropriation of technology to include all forms of theatre production and media. Rather than set a predetermined political agenda that roots our work, we prefer to explore whatever discipline necessary to best communicate the ideas of the project we are exploring. We deliberately try 'old' and 'new' forms and techniques and try to let the work 'tell us' how it's best realised.

Despite our deliberately eclectic approach to making work, we do have a methodology, or 'technique', or set of inclinations, preoccupations and common media/methods, that we draw from often. In this recycling of form and medium we obviously get more and more skilled and accomplished. With this also comes new languages and vocabularies, and a way of talking and communicating that assumes a mutual understanding of things. Like many other collectives and companies/troupes (wherever you want to call them), over the years we have developed a shorthand for things. Shortcuts, colloquialisms, slang, crude labels, aphorisms, keywords... all of which help us work more economically and simply 'in the room'. "Shit-good" is one of these terms. Basically it means "('it' is) so shit, it's good". We originally used it to describe bad movies we loved. Kitsch, B-Movies, or those particular films with super-bad (over-earnest, poorly scripted) 'acting' in them. It slid into our performance making parlance by accident. If you have B-Movies, then it surely goes that you have "B-Theatre". There was a moment when we realised that a lot of our work employed rudimentary, analogue, 'lo-fi' mediums and aesthetics. We'd always shied away from the mainstream, and as such It's something we'd been doing as a matter of course for many years ourselves. Not out of any political agenda or aesthetic inclination, but because we made work with little or no money.

Over the years we've...

...achieved "Bullet time" by turning really slowly in a slightly moving action pose, made a time machine using a Tomy child's steering wheel and a rainbow-coloured umbrella,

made (stick puppet) ants crawl over a 2ft (polystyrene) hand, made Kubrick-esque corridors tilt by slightly twisting a square tube of Lycra, helped an army of (cheap plastic) soldiers march to war. We reached space by climbing a ladder. Got to a show by walking there (it was 500 miles away), recreated an entire film using cardboard, gaffer tape, toys and a table. We've helped others channel Bob Ross and release their inner artist (Bob, after all, tells us that "we are all artists"), built stages on the back of tricycles... we've done hi-tech things in lo-tech ways and visa versa.

There's something about "shit-good" and "B-Theatre" that rings true for a lot of DIY theatre and performance. Though, like B-Movies, it's not just about deliberately crude aesthetics. Economics is certainly a key factor. For us it is at least. We are not commercially driven as a company, but we do need money to make work. And there's very little of it to go around. We make work with very small budgets, and make no real profit by touring. So, for us, to employ a DIY approach is to make this apparent 'weakness' a virtue. Anne Bogart reminds us that "Within the framework of art and theater you will find a special freedom and the space and time to explore complexities. It does not cost you anything. It costs you your life." (2007: 11). Many like us, and before us, are similarly sanguine and embracing of this economic (and philosophical) situation. Recognising that the only 'cost' is the time and space we give it, and that the quality of the 'art' is not concomitant with the quantity of money (or anything else) spent on it. But herein lies a problem. Many young artists are beginning to adopt the symbolic forms and methodologies of ethos without fully understanding the socio-political, economic and cultural contexts and conditions in which they were initially constructed. So instead of artists making lo-fi work because they have to, work is now being made deliberately 'cheap', as if its a trend, as opposed to a socio-economic predicament.

And what you get - as Abigail Conway put to me in her initial response to the call out for this book - is, "that it is nearly always considered to be low fi - with little or poor production values. This of course, in most cases, serves a purpose and has been ingrained into many of us by our

DIY forefathers. I would argue however, that DIY, even though learnt on the job - can also be - specific, beautiful and highly stylised- and still be rooted in DIY approaches to theatre/ live art making... (small rant over)."

And I hope that some of what this book does is to properly crack this issue. At its worst young artists are using a DIY ethos and style as an excuse to not care about craftsmanship or rigour, when in fact it should simply imply (and exploit) more rudimentary, accessible, tools and media, and promote being more self-reliant. In a way, 'lo-fi' isn't about under-producing work/material (etc.) but just not over-producing it: simply resisting the sycophantic commercial hegemony.

There's also an assumption made about many artists and collectives, and some aspects of the DIY scene, that it is - or can be - elitist. Or worse: esoteric. The 'reach' of this work is limited and the places where it is often presented belonging to exclusive communities and networks. I hope some of the contributions in this book help demystify these assumptions.

This viewpoint is not without relevance, and there have been some well presented arguments that critique the parochial remit of style and 'permitted' socio-political (and aesthetic) agenda. And like the punk movement, and the inherent dichotomy it had between its socio-political ethos and its aesthetic symbolism, DIY performance is sometimes similarly confused: those that embrace the ethos, and those that adopt (mimic) the 'style'. The latter being what many critics of this scene tend to focus on: a bunch of (middle class, playing poor) self-serving, hipster elitists making work too entrenched in superficial and esoteric knowledges. Many new DIY-aligned artists and art is self-congratulatory. Young (or not so young!) people trying so hard to stay 'zeit', to be 'cool'; riding their vintage bicycle to work, in charity-shop clothes and beat-up hair, decrying the 'Mainstream' as evil and oppressive, or that being 'Commercial' is 'selling out'. Same story, different era. The punks did this. So too the Dadaists and Situationists. And they became the very establishment they sought to revolt against.

Of course some of what happens is self-serving. It has to be! When commercial and mainstream structures prevent and inhibit the assimilation of independent movements, they can only continue on their own terms. There's no 'inside and outside - its all fluid. "The "community" is made up of whoever is hanging out and producing work. If you're hanging out and going to shows and you're spending time on the couch - you're in - if you're not, you're not." (Smith in Biel, 2012: 52) and so it can be said that if one feels 'excluded' from the community, or feel it needs to shift, then they should simply join in and shift it. The one thing DIY organisations and communities can attest to and celebrate is their willingness to include, develop organically and be 'whoever makes up the numbers at the time'. Forest Fringe is one such example. With nuclear family of Deborah Pearson, Andy Field and now Ira Brand too, the wider family has never been the same. A fundamentally fluid and amorphous corpus.

In many ways the mainstream (commercial) arts sector is the exclusive, elitist, ivory tower, not the small, 'alternative' or even esoteric communities and collectives. It's arcane and monolithic class system is choking the very life out of theatre and performance. Like a true patriarchy. It's comforting to note, that whilst the mainstream, commercial sector is hegemonic and all-assimilating, it is NOT the common form. Put simply, there are more of us than there are of them. It is DIY cultures, communities and its followers that form part of a viable antithesis to capitalist, mainstream media (and the UK theatre establishment especially) that is woefully archaic and resistant to such fluid change.

And it's in this wider cultural context that many of the contributors to this book look to create a dialogue with. As James - my friend and co-artistic director - mentioned when we initially discussed my ideas for this book; "For me the culture of DIY is less about being counter-cultural per se, but instead about finding creative ways in which hegemonic power structures can be manipulated and shaped to benefit the small artist/collective. As an artist I don't want to sit outside of society looking in, I want to be what (I think) Joseph Kosuth terms an anthropologist engaged". You can read more from James later.

His position offers a refreshing antithesis to my own perspective. I think many included in this book would completely agree. The main reason I wanted to make this book is because I wanted to give voice to a kind of performance making I feel is important to recognise. Whether its my perspective, one of the other authors in this book, or one of the many voices not included: whatever this is it can't be ignored any further. Artists and collectives that follow a DIY ethos and style has been poking and provoking the mainstream for many years, though we're so locked into an archaic system that even when the odd happening bursts to life and galvanises a sense of place and progression in the homogenous mainstream it is quickly dubbed 'alternative', 'fringe', or worse 'experimental' (to say the least) and elitist: we are quickly ostracised and marginalised.

It made sense to pool together a bunch of people and make an effort to snapshot the phenomenon and community. There was a conscious choice to self-publish too. With support from The University of Chichester (where I teach) and The Live Art Development Agency's Unbound bookstore I've managed to provide a simple infrastructure and format for people to contribute. I've done it myself. Or rather: we are doing it together, which James, who I've already cited, will also talk more about later in this book.

So why a book? First of all, (self)publishing is at the heart of any DIY ethos and history. It has given voice and credence to the beat poets and science fiction writers of the pre and post war world, it has helped galvanise communities and sub-cultures in 'indie' music, and provided foundation and opportunity for artists to integrate into established and protective sectors (like the way in which higher education in the UK - at least - is welcoming of artists such as myself, enabling me to continue making work free from doctrine or dictate of mediocre 'public support' criteria). A book is simply a part of the wider network of dissemination. Publishing is analogous to a modern-day patronage. And, I would argue, it's still a crucial element to any non-mainstream, alternative, or 'counter-cultural' community. In theatre and performance, online 'zines' such as Exeunt, Zite,

Zealous, Total Theatre and Bellyflop (to mention just the few that I read on a regular basis) are important aspects to independent artists and collectives. They give exposure and promotion to those whom the mainstream media overlook and ignore. Before them; Performance (Magazine), Hybrid, Live Art Magazine and the Mime Action Group's MAGazine. Like our predecessors, we are a community, or scene, We are a scene documenting itself: like the fly posting and mass-printed art of the Pop..', Dadaist, situationist and fluxus movements, as well as the "zines" of the beat writers, and punks before us. In fact it's in these open-source platforms where we can see a real rumbling of revolution and paradigm shift. Only platforms and environments like the Internet have shifted this problem: and it's (apparently) ability to widen the immediacy and reach of non-mainstream. These media platforms, the World Wide Web itself, can be seen as a constantly evolving kinetic or visual 'zine'. With a much wider reach.

These predecessors can be seen as the Promethean figures of the Art world in the way their posters, documents and mass-printed work "were designed to change the widely held perception of art as elitist and instead establish the idea that it could be universal and accessible (Spencer, 2008: 100). Whilst I wouldn't dare claim that this book is as profoundly important to the wider world, I do hope that it echoes a similar effort to provide fora and platform for readers to get a better insight and understanding of a mode of production, and way of life, that has been innovating and revolutionising the way in which art can be made, enjoyed and perceived for many years already.

And if it isn't this publication or the blogs, articles and documents that came before it - of which there are many - can at least be seen in way some venues, festivals and artist-led collectives and cooperatives help landmark and cohere disparate groups. Shunt, Forest Fringe, STK, Residence...even the original ethos of the Edinburgh Fringe Festival: there are a number of venues, festivals and "DiY" organisations where one might see such inter-artistic practices. Even though it still retains its counter-cultural and anti-hegemonic ideologies, DIY theatre and performance can no longer be seen as an 'alternative' practice, or artistic sub-culture. There is a demonstrably tangible zeitgeist and - concerning the people taking the time to contribute this book: a volksgeist - with a growing number of 'micro-festivals', mutually supportive collectives, 'pop-up' venues, happenings and events to compliment the network of landmark organisations and venues, it's possible to speculate that where we are right now is in the early stages of a major paradigm shift in theatre production and its connection to society and culture. It may take some time for any shift to happen but with the continued activity of the myriad artists, collectives, organisations and venues continuing to thrive in spite of a socio-economic crisis we are demonstrating that 'other' ways of making art, and connecting with audiences are not just viable but demonstrably more successful than the the established models. A which is, I would argue, desperately perpetuated by an out-of-tune class system, bloated, archaic and barely relevant to young people, and modern culture and society.

Perhaps with this book and ones like it, the generous and continued action of the artists involved and those in the wider community who are yet to be given voice but work tirelessly and independently to take new theatre and performance to audiences of all kinds, people might begin to see that 'doing it yourself' is not only a viable alternative to the hackneyed tradition, but a vital one. The more we can welcome others to join us on this mission - not by 'fitting in' (where preceding revolts have suffered by their lack of fluidity) but by embracing diversity and heterogeneity - the more versatile and dimensional it will become. Strength only in numbers and the ability to evolve as fluidly as time itself.

This is just a beginning of something.

by Robert Daniels

Bibliography

Biel, J. (2012) *Beyond the Music: How Punks are saving the World with DIY ethics, Skills & Values*, CantankerousTitles.com: Portland

Bogart, A. (2007) *And then, you act. making art in an unpredictable world*, Routledge: New York DIY 10: 2013

http://www.thisisliveart.co.uk/prof_dev/diy/diy_10_index.dwt

Halfacree, Keith (2004) *I Could Only Do Wrong': Academic Research and DiY Culture* (unpublished article, available at: http://www.praxis-epress.org/rtcp/kh.pdf) (Date accessed: 17/07/2013)

Heddon, D. and Klein, K. (eds. 2012) *Histories and Practices of Live Art*, Palgrave Macmillan: London

McKay, G. (ed. 1998) *DIY Culture - Party and Protest in Nineties Britain*, Verso: London.

Nicklin, H (2011) *DIY Music and DIY theatre* (unpublished article, available at: http://www.hannahnicklin.com/2011/12/diy-music-and-diy-theatre) (Date accessed: 13/09/2013)

Nicklin, H (2011) *Music and theatre should belong to nobody, everybody*, (unpublished article, available at: http://ilivesweat. tumblr.com/post/13838799382/music-and-theatre-should-belong-to-nobody-everybody (Date accessed: 18/07/2013)

Spencer, A. (2008) *DIY: The Rise of Lo-Fi Culture*, Marion Boyars: London

Stenhouse, J. (2011) in Nicklin, H (2011) *DIY Music and DIY theatre* (unpublished article, available at: http://www.hannahnicklin.com/2011/12/diy-music-and-diy-theatre/) (Date accessed: 18/07/2013)

Gob Squad and A. Quinõnes (eds) (2005) *The Making of a Memory: 10 Years of Gob Squad Remembered in Words and Pictures*, Synwolt Verlag: Berlin

The
CONTRIBUTORS

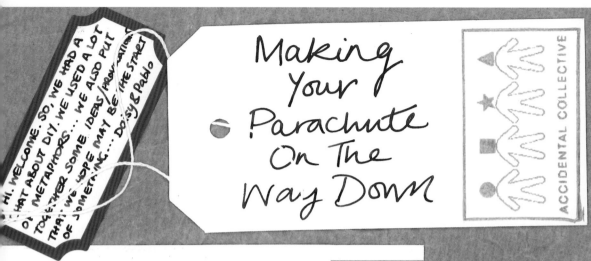

Making Your Parachute On The Way Down

HI, WELCOME. SO, WE HAD A LOT THAT ABOUT DIY. WE USED A LOT OF METAPHORS... WE ALSO PUT TOGETHER SOME IDEAS/PROVOCATIONS THAT WE HOPE MAY BE THE START OF SOMETHING... Daisy & Pablo

ACCIDENTAL COLLECTIVE

D: DIY. Do. It. Yourself.

P: Is it an imperative or an invitation?

D: Maybe that's the beauty about it. Maybe there's space for both in DIY performance. Either one provokes action.

P: Yes, it enables things to happen in ways, in contexts, in spaces where they might not otherwise happen. In that way, DIY is like a type of weed, it flowers in the most unexpected places. And in making things happen, it widens the crevices and creates a space for future growth.

D: Do It Yourself. Make Things Happen... If I got a tattoo I'd consider that.

D: For me DIY is like a suitcase full of stuff. It's the kit, the tools everybody has, the things everybody has lying around that - should they wish to - they could make a piece of performance with.

P: It's the POSSIBILITIES. A bit of string, some post-its, an old broom... All the possibilities they offer.

D: DIY is all about multiplicity, there's never a singular solution. The power of 'it' (in do 'it' yourself) is precisely that 'it' can be *many* things.

P: And unlike the DIY of home improvements or self-assembly furniture, DIY in performance-making does not prescribe or allow for ready-made solutions.

START ANYWHERE

D: There's this idea that DIY is thrown together or does not involve skill...

P: Well there's also that 'look' that seems to say "I don't really care".

D: Yeah and I think that something's changed and that people *do* want to see 'CARE' in all senses of the word. Like, "I have put this together with CARE and I CARE about you".

P: Aesthetically I see a continuum, from the somewhat slapdash to the still handmade but more carefully crafted...

DON'T WAIT FOR PERMISSION.
DON'T WAIT FOR AN AUDIENCE.

D: I don't think we *became* DIY. When we began we just wanted to make work, so we didn't wait around - we just did it. Of course the circumstances had a bearing...

P: Yes, the time and location were extremely important. East Kent circa 2005/6 was not the place it is now. I sometimes do think that we 'fell' into the work we did and do. We did not perform in theatres because the cultural landscape at the time was not ready. So we went outside those spaces. We made pieces that were specific to a setting, community, event... We invited people to participate in our work or interact with us out of a desire to find an audience and/or make one for ourselves, to meet people half way. We were the first company that stayed in East Kent after graduating. So we helped kick-start a new generation of Kent-based performance makers. All along we have been very active in supporting others on their own way: in connecting people, in establishing a 'scene', in providing platforms and opportunities for our peers... We are doing it ourselves. Because we had to, because we want to.

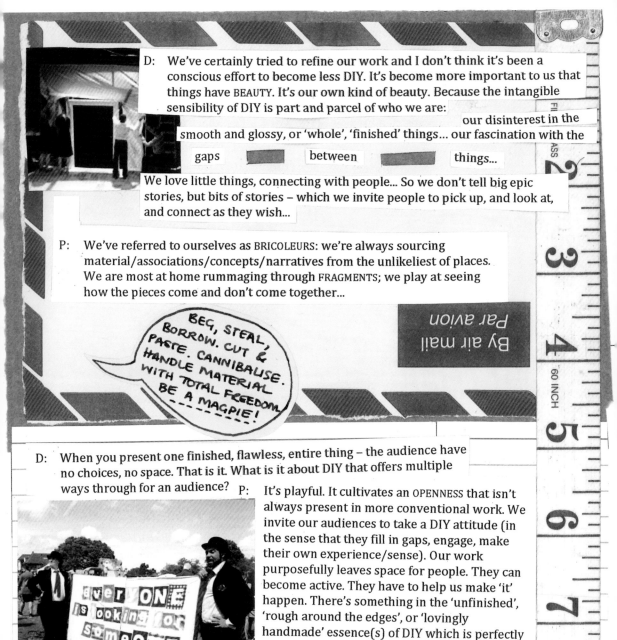

D: We've certainly tried to refine our work and I don't think it's been a conscious effort to become less DIY. It's become more important to us that things have BEAUTY. It's our own kind of beauty. Because the intangible sensibility of DIY is part and parcel of who we are: our disinterest in the smooth and glossy, or 'whole', 'finished' things... our fascination with the gaps between things...

We love little things, connecting with people... So we don't tell big epic stories, but bits of stories – which we invite people to pick up, and look at, and connect as they wish...

P: We've referred to ourselves as BRICOLEURS: we're always sourcing material/associations/concepts/narratives from the unlikeliest of places. We are most at home rummaging through FRAGMENTS; we play at seeing how the pieces come and don't come together...

BEG, STEAL, BORROW. CUT & PASTE. CANNIBALISE. HANDLE MATERIAL WITH TOTAL FREEDOM. BE A MAGPIE!

By air mail
Par avion

D: When you present one finished, flawless, entire thing – the audience have no choices, no space. That is it. What is it about DIY that offers multiple ways through for an audience?

P: It's playful. It cultivates an OPENNESS that isn't always present in more conventional work. We invite our audiences to take a DIY attitude (in the sense that they fill in gaps, engage, make their own experience/sense). Our work purposefully leaves space for people. They can become active. They have to help us make 'it' happen. There's something in the 'unfinished', 'rough around the edges', or 'lovingly handmade' essence(s) of DIY which is perfectly suited to enable the experiences we want to create.

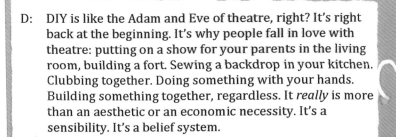

D: DIY is like the Adam and Eve of theatre, right? It's right back at the beginning. It's why people fall in love with theatre: putting on a show for your parents in the living room, building a fort. Sewing a backdrop in your kitchen. Clubbing together. Doing something with your hands. Building something together, regardless. It *really* is more than an aesthetic or an economic necessity. It's a sensibility. It's a belief system.

COMMIT YOURSELF TO EXPLORE. FIND OR INVENT A SOLUTION THAT FITS.

CONSIDER YOUR LIMITATIONS. EMBRACE THEM, OVERCOME THEM, BYPASS THEM.

BUILD A FORT!

YOU DON'T HAVE TO PLAY BY THE SAME RULES...

AN INVITATION

Start at home. Let your eye wander over the things around you. Make a selection (colour, texture, size, associations). Get a suitcase or a bag. Put a couple of things into it. Pick a space, pick a time. Walk there. Collect a few more things along the way (rummage through skips if you have to). Arrive. Look. Land. This is your stage. Lay out your materials in whichever fashion seems appropriate. Realise your performance has already begun; just carry on. Discover rules along the way...

1) Tell a story. 2) Tell no story. 3) Make a poem. 4) Make a sculpture. 5) Make a confession. 6) Make an interaction.

LET YOUR DESIRE TO MAKE OVER-RULE PRACTICALITY OR DOUBT.

DON'T GIVE UP.

DO SOMETHING

1.   The first thing we <u>did</u> as a collaboration was book a flight to Kaoshiung in Taiwan.

2.   We were following the reasoning that to <u>do</u> that would be better than to not do that.

3.   We were invited there by a man called Tony Chen. We met him at university. His mother and father owned a restaurant in Taiwan and he used to cook lavish meals in our student halls with strange crustaceans hed bought at Leeds market. He was a research student and we worked with him on his projects. He directed us in 3 performances. Strange, beautiful, spectacularly experimental performances. His one and only instruction at nearly all stages of the process (infuriatingly for 19 year old drama students) was, <u>do something</u>.

4.   After graduating James worked as a labourer and decided he didnt want to be an actor or make theatre anymore. Gemma worked for some Theatre in Education companies, a kind of right of passage for recent graduates at the time. Then James broke both his legs at work in a freak accident. He lay on a sofa unable to move (or put his own socks on) for 3 months. We ran out of money, we lived in a council estate in Wakefield in a house with no central heating. We decided we had to <u>do something</u>. So we sold all our possessions (an old stereo, a guitar and a table) and bought two tickets to Taiwan.

5.   We arrived in Tainan City with no money, no job and nowhere to live. We found a school that would let us teach English without any proper teaching qualifications and they sorted out a visa for us. For the next 12 months we taught English fulltime to keep our visa and worked with Tony on the evenings and weekends. Every night the first thing we <u>did</u> when we arrived in the rehearsal room was mop the floor.

6.   Tony was making a show called Messland. None of the performers were professional (there is very little professional experimental theatre in Taiwan) and most of them spoke no English at all. Rehearsals were in Mandarin. Which was ok because the only instruction was <u>do something</u>.

7.   We quickly realized that we were at a slight advantage to the other performers by not understanding what was being said. Trying to understand, trying to find out what Tony wanted, trying to know what we were supposed to be doing was not helpful to the process. By being continuously in the dark we were liberated by accepting the fact that we were unlikely to know why we were doing anything, so all that was left to <u>do</u> was <u>something</u>.

8.   You can place the emphasis on the <u>do</u> or the <u>something</u> and either way its a profound manifesto for making performance.

9.   Tony Chen works in a bookstore in Tainan City. We havent seen him in person since we left, but every now and then if were stuck in a process racking our brains for a decent idea/paralysed by a failed funding bid/sobbing in a rehearsal room because the pressure is killing us, well think about mopping floors/drinking bubble tea/riding scooters and shows with a slow-mo dolphin balloon/a man with a pot on his head /a performance where everythingisinMandarinandyouvenoideawhatsgoingonandyoureintheshow, and we remember all we have to <u>Do</u> is <u>Something</u>.

What's (s)he BUILDING in there?
What the hell is (s)he BUILDING in there?

Tom Waits

CANNONBALLISTA

This script (work in progress excert) was recorded as a soundscape with the fantastic voice of Ed Rapley. If perhaps you know him, imagine the following read in his best showmanly tones…

Ladies & Gentlemen (because that's how it always starts)… You are here tonight to witness an amazing, an incredible and a death defying feat.

She's a renegade mechanic, an altruistic megalomaniac, the mistress of contradiction herself ladies and gentlemen. I give you the new and improved. 50% extra extra, one woman husband and wife team…

SMALL CANNON. DOLL BIT (drum roll)

He told her she was short! Folks, she's an impressive 5'9 (she unveils Barbie)

He told her she'd never achieve! (she unveils cannon)

He told her not to bother…!' (she puts Barbie's hands above head)

Ladies & Gentlemen, I give you MS BETTY BRUISER! (shoots Barbie out of cannon)

Applause

MEDIUM CANNON

OK ladies & gents, a little bit of quiet now as Betty climbs into the cannon. I'm sure you'll understand that we can't reveal the exact mechanics of how far into the barrel she climbs. Needless to say it's a very technical feat. The angle of elevation is a precise science ladies and gentlemen; calculated by Betty's own method. Betty's physical training methods ladies & gentlemen are of course extremely unorthodox and entirely unsafe. She has been thrown out of cannon club for breaking the first rule of cannon club- revealing too much…

OK, now we have elevation (BEEP BEEP BEEP) OK, now we're at about 22 degrees and climbing. We're about half way there. OK ladies & gentlemen. Please. The cannon is at the optimum angle. All systems go. (DRUM ROLL as Betty wheels on the cannon)

Fade 1.18.

BIG CANNON

So ladies & gentlemen. Betty built this cannon. She has built 3 in total now. Not to mention one monster truck and a fleet of diamond encrusted diggers. Her workshop is in the backyard of her Bristol semi, where she also practices her jumps. No one knows exactly what's in that shed of hers but there's been a lot of speculation including 'Time Machine', 'Nazi Regalia' & 'Hovercraft'. Ladies & gentlemen; who knows.

Just while we are waiting for Betty to ascend the barrel of the cannon here are some interesting facts…

Soft rock

• It has been built with super industrial strength materials, strong enough to withstand any external attack; lovingly rendered by Ms Bruiser herself.

• The highly sought after & extremely rare blend of explosives is Betty's own personal recipe, handed down to her by… No one. So ladies & gents you are in safe hands tonight.

• The mechanics & technicalities of this feat are of course Top Secret. So seriously does Betty take this responsibility that they are at all times secreted about her person

• On that note ladies & gentlemen Betty would like you to know that her outfit matches the cannon at all times

• OK, a signal from Betty there that she is nearly ready & that a few final safety checks are needed

1 min pause

(superman rolling bit)Ladies & Gentlemen. The moment you've all been waiting for. Can I just remind you to please maintain a safe distance from the Cannon. For Betty's safety and for yours. Well, actually, just yours. Join me, ladies and gentlemen, if you will please in our COUNTDOWN! (superman!)

5
4
3
2
1

EXPLOSION. JUMP. GLITTER

HI ... IM LIZ

I'm a live artist, performance maker, whatever. I have been making performance for over 10 years on and off. I am a mother with two children under five. It has been in these last five years that I have embraced my practice and focused on making work with I guess what you would call a DIY ethos. This for me has been a natural choice borne out of necessity; but also about identifying with the 'Other', with the lowbrow, with always searching and finding joy in the performance thing that you stumble upon in the multistory, in the bar, in the cupboard under the stairs. It is here for me that the 'real' experiences lie. Betty Bruiser, the anti-heroine of the above excerpt is a snake charming, bar room brawling, highbrow lowlife alter ego who sometimes jostles in on my performance making.

The text is from a new piece inspired by working for the last five years with women with mental health issues through my company Drastic Productions. The action takes place in the SHED OF BETTY'S MIND to which the audience are invited. On the stage, construction of the shiny hardware progresses, with bravado, with gusto, with song and with several costume changes; down amongst the audience, through a more vulnerable showing of the Self we witness the inner workings of a woman on the edge of something. I wanted to share it with you as it physically embodies my DIY approach. A shambolic construction of something new and unexpected takes place, engineered by the performer out of something mundane and ordinary. It's low tech, physical work. Pig's ear silk purse-y. My metaphoric cannon!

This beloved Betty Blaster has gone through several incarnations; a silver toilet roll covered with tissue paper stars; a disused container big enough to climb into (once housing something very minty which stays stuck in your hair for weeks); and an intricate, deadly contraption made from an old trampoline, a water butt and a Zimmer frame (Sadly dismantled when space under the stairs became at a premium for storing cribs and baby gyms rather than pyrotechnic paraphernalia).

So, a lot of my work is about construction. Construction of a Self, an image, an Icon. It examines the constructs of the Feminine and how this impossible image crumbles. The cannon metaphor, with its phallic symbolism suggests trappings of male dominated war mongering. Another of my performances 'Construction Site' invites an audience to layer on costume and make up to construct a hideous version of a female; the hyper feminine, the Drag of a Drag of a Drag which is then let loose on stage in an improvised performance.

My work has developed significantly in the last year with the support of Arnolfini. This support has enabled me to take risks, make mess, get tattooed in their basement and prance around inside a 6 foot balloon on their premises. Their approach of 'Let's go for it and see what happens' has given me confidence in my work and my place in the whole mishmash of a 'cultural landscape.'

The organisation is also supporting an 18 month project with Drastic Productions, the not for profit company I run which uses live art and performance as a framework to work with women with mental health issues; enabling them to take supported risks in performance and create new, bold work. Arnolfini is supporting the project by providing studio space for the group to meet weekly. Working with the Arnolfini gives an added sense of pride and ownership to the participants who feel welcome in an arts establishment they may not have had the opportunity to engage with previously.

DP does things that shouldn't be allowed in 'proper theatre', that give voice to women (sometimes celebratory, sometimes primal and unattractive - heaven forefend!) It has been said that we are 'Better than six years of therapy' and 'Should be on the NHS' (go figure).

Our approach has always been anarchic and independent, railing against the traditional community theatre that I witnessed in the past. I'd leave a theatre or community hall with a deep sense of embarrassment and anger on behalf of the participants who had been shoved on stage in an ill fitting costume and given a line to read out. Having worked on the front line of mental health and homelessness services and with domestic violence charities I knew that people had far more valuable and interesting contributions to make and that exploring these experiences through the prism of performance in a responsible and safe way was something really exciting. In the current project the women have embarked on a performance process to unlock their 'super hero alter ego'. They will then commission a graphic novelist to transform their work into print. The DIY approach to making artwork gives participants a sense of freedom and joy in addition to ownership and group solidarity. This way of working is accessible and friendly and by allowing people to enter into a DIY process opens up something in themselves; a confidence to create, to take risks and make some truly amazing work.

Image credit: Jeremy Horwood

AMAZE

A History Of DIY Successes And Failures In The Life Of Pat Ashe

This is a inaccurate and incomplete attempt to map the history of DIY projects that have formed my thinking behind DIY performance both projects I have done and ones I have witnessed

I'm going begin this history of my DIY life with a moment which I feel sums up a DIY approach to performance/theatre/art/life. It's a dull Friday morning and I'm stood on the deck of MS Stubniz an ageing East German fishing trawler docked in the beating heart of capitalism that is Canary Wharf. Around in the shiny buildings are people pushing unimaginable amounts of money around the world for the benefit of very few people. The boat sits in the water, bobbing up and down. People are beginning to arrive for *Bit Of Alright*, a games conference that is happening on this grey boat on this grey morning. It's a mix of talks, provocations, games, tea, workshops and just the general chit chat you get at conferences. But before we can descend into the bowels of the ship, we've got to queue up in the mid May drizzle and get our wristbands. As we are queuing up, one of the people showing their game today is busy sawing away at some old blue pallets in the corner of the deck. 30 minutes later and these pallets have been reborn as the Splintercade, a bold blue centrepiece for the games area with people crowding round all day. According to Jonatan Van Hove, the guy who built both the arcade and co-created the game being shown *LAZA KNITEZ!!*, this arcade cabinet cost nothing to make. All the tools were borrowed and the materials given for free by friends and friends of friends. The next day Jonatan will be show his game *GO NUTS!!* at the The Wild Rumpus, a multiplayer games night, and again the Splintercade will be a centrepiece for the evening. The Splintercade was born from a need to follow through an idea, put together thanks to a community willing to share, enjoyed by people who had no idea how this thing was

born before being thrown in a skip somewhere around Canary Wharf never to be seen again. This is what DIY is to me and this is an article about how I came to understand what DIY was.

2005. Ashby School. I've just formed a band. Me and Dom Kidson have just become *Porpoise Queen*. This is just the latest in a long line of bands formed by the teenage Ashe children. From *FX15* to *Pobel* to *Asbestos Lung* to *The J Funk Explosion* to *The Haze* and finally to *Porpoise Queen*. Formed in the room round the back of the music department, PQ were born out of the marriage of DIY ethics and the love of messing about on synthesizers. I even built my own keytar out of a cheap keyboard bought at a car boot as I couldn't afford a proper one for a few months. The original plan was to make a series of EPs, one each month for a year and sell them for the exact amount it cost to make the EPs, a grand total of about 40p. Only one of these EP was made, the bizarrely titled '*You'll Find Me In Office C*' as well the rare one off pressing of that EP called '*Porpoise Queen: No Frills More Thrills*'. After this EP was recorded in one afternoon, printed and at least 30 copies were sold around school to our mates we moved on to our next record. The record that in many ways would define us and break us, we left the Months EP series behind us, a failed experiment, and started work on '*The End Of The Man*'. A concept album about a dystopian nightmare world where an ordinary man driven insane by his soul destroying work and his useless possessions attempts to destroy the Man. Again we burnt the CDs ourselves, printed the artwork on my parent's printer and sold them for 40p at school. Again we sold around 20-30 copies. After the success of *The End Of The Man*, we moved onto bigger projects like playing live. We played a total of 4 gigs. One at our mate Pete's birthday, where Dom had to work a double shift at McDonald's and couldn't make it so I played all the instruments myself and the DJ put music over the top of me after one song. The next was a gig at our mate Leanne's house party, this was a guerilla gig where we played a set on kitchen utensils. Following this we performed a gig at my house when my parent's were out of town. This was a much more organised gig where both Me and Dom were there and had our instruments set up, amplified and at least 6 people were there to listen to us. After this gig, I gave my mate Tuffen a best of called '*All Fresh Hits*' featuring all the tracks off our first two CDs and some unreleased tracks we'd recorded with our mate Kier Forbes on bass. This was the last release Porpoise

Queen ever made. The final gig that Porpoise Queen ever played was a surprise gig at a house party (can't remember whose) where I played a set of songs to a couple of people before accidentally hitting my friend Chris in the face with the unamplifed electric guitar I was playing which I then threw on the roof thus marking the end of Porpoise Queen. Shortly after this Myspace deleted our page and all the tracks up on it were lost forever. Only the tracks from *You'll Find Me In Office C* and *The End Of The Man* survive. No documentation of any gigs we played survive.

We Want Your Dog was a performance night started by me, James Allum, Leonie MacDonald and during the final one Megan McCarter. It was born from a frustration at a lack of a performance culture in our university town and a way of saving ourselves the train fare to London and beyond every other week when we wanted to go see performances. We ran 3 nights whilst we were active, the first two in the back room of a music pub in Winchester where we had a mix of local acts from our university, ourselves and other performers we knew in the local area perform. These first two nights were a success (i.e. we paid back the pub for the hire and made a little bit of money on top of that). There were a few setbacks like the pub getting our name wrong in all their advertising for the first night, instead of *We Want Your Dog* we went out in their flyers as *We Wank Your Dog*, and us booking the second night for the week after everyone at uni had gone home for the summer. We had good friendly crowds, we felt like this was something we could build on to create something special. For the 3rd night we moved to a bigger venue (a studio theatre rather than the back room of a pub) to try some new ideas out, spread our wings and see what we could do. We booked a London-based performer to come down and do a scratch of his new show, we got posters printed up, we were going to smash it at our new venue. For a variety of reasons the 3rd night was a success and a failure. It was the best night of performance we'd had but at the same time fewer people came along compared to previous nights and with the cost of bringing a performer down from London and a new venue that cost more we lost money and we had to pay the gap out of our own cash. Soon after this we disbanded having done 3 fantastic nights of crazy, wonky, ramshackle performance pulled together by 4 people with no real clue how to run a performance night.

Ut Astrum Una Hora: Or How To Get To The Stars In Under An Hour was created for the final year of my undergraduate study at Winchester University. It was created in conjunction with Kris Rowland, James Allum, Victoria Henry and Megan McCarter. With our budget of £100 we set about creating space in the Arts Centre of Winchester University. Using hand made shadow puppets, a variety of borrowed, broken and 2nd hand torches and lamps, a tent covered in tin foil and a few pot plants we created a show about space, distance, loneliness and the five of us being locked into a small space for months on end. The show used none of our theatre spaces technical elements as all lights and sound element were created by either us the performers or by the audience who had been equipped with torches and lamps at the start of the performance. We aimed to give the audience the agency to light us, move around as they wanted and to work with us to create this performance. We pushed ourselves throughout the performance to try new things out that we had no experience of such as creating and using shadow puppets and to create a open and welcome space to experiment in for both us the performers and also for the audience. This show was DIY through necessity due to our scope and our budget but we decided early on to not let these limit us in any real way and to use the DIY elements of our performance as the core of all our thinking and creation practices. We wanted to take our audience to space in an old studio theatre and so the only way to do this was to build it ourselves.

For the last ever *We Want Your Dog* night that we ran I created a performance called *Several Amazing Things About Tetris* (1984), it was a short performance lecture about Tetris and my relationship with the game. From this original version I've created several different incarnations until April 2013 when I performed the show for the last time. The main form the piece took was a 20 minute performance lecture close to the original version but the performance only lasted as long as 1 person could keep playing Tetris on a NES for. This meant the show could last from between 1 minute to the full 20 if a player was good enough. It also meant the show could be performed as a 1-on-1 piece as well as a more traditional piece. The piece was created so that it all fitted into my backpack apart from my TV which I just carried and thus was performable in a variety of spaces throughout it's life. From stairwells to stages to booths to 7 hour long performances in tents to it's final outing on a rickety stage in Berlin *Several Amazing Things About Tetris* (1984) was rejigged, adapted and staged in all manner of places in all manner of ways and was the first solo show I made that really fitted into my idea of DIY making at that time.

After *Several Amazing Things About Tetris* (1984) was a 'finished' show I moved on to my next solo project *An Oasis In 5 Parts*. This was a show about my home town spilt into 5 parts. Each part was meant to be a new form that I'd not created work in before or a taking a new approach to my previous work in that form. Part 1 was a performance piece, part 2 was an audio piece, part 3 was a video game, part 4 was a performance for cinema spaces and part 5 was a zine created from interviews and bits of the previous parts that were cut or discarded during the making process. Throughout the development of these 5 parts I strove to maintain certain approaches to the work as I had done in previous shows and so the shows were on the whole tech light and could be toured in 1 suitcase. The 5 parts all worked as separate pieces but when brought together built into a whole show which like my previous show meant the 5 pieces could easily be shown in a variety of performance situations and allowed to grow and change depending on where they were being performed. The ability to change, adapt and react to a space is a key component in DIY work for me as performing the same show over and over again can become dull but always adapting means every show is unique and playful.

Midnight at Victoria Coach Station waiting for the long slow Megabus up to Edinburgh for the Fringe. I won't sleep one bit on that coach, the guy next to me will fall asleep onto me, it'll be too dark to read but as the sun rises over the sea as we wind our way up to Scotland it'll all seem worth it. I've not got anywhere to sleep yet, I booked my coach ticket about 24 hours ago. I've been unemployed for nearly 5 months and am living hand to mouth but there was no way I was going to miss this Edinburgh Fringe. This is the last year the Forest Café and Forest Fringe are in their old leaky, cold yet majestic church hall before they are kicked out for other people's mistakes. I couldn't not be there. It's about 7 in the morning when I step off the bus and wander down from Prince's Street to find the church hall locked up. I sit down and wait for the Forest Café to open, once it does I grab a tea and try and shake off the lack of sleep. I chat to a guy who has hitch-hiked all the way from

Canada to Edinburgh and crashed behind some bushes last night. No sleep on a Megabus seems quite good now. Eventually Andy Field and Debbie Pearson, the co-artistic directors turn up and we get to work turning the church hall upstairs into a usable performance space for the last ever August Forest Fringe will spend in Bristo Place. The first day is mostly spent battling with a giant wooden cake that the Forest Café built to celebrate their 10th birthday the night before. It sits balanced on top of the old pulpit right above the stage of the hall. It's got to be taken down, Andy clambers on top of the cake clutching a hammer and begins to tear the cake apart. Wood, nails and bit of cake decorations fall around whilst we pick up empty beer bottles and plastic glasses. Soon the cake has been torn down, swept up and put in the bin. In it's place is the Forest Fringe for the next two weeks, the cake is soon forgotten and then the Forest Fringe packs up and leaves. Finally on the 31st the community that is the Forest leaves it's home. Bristo Place ends up like the wooden cake. Oh and I found somewhere to crash that was better than the bushes.

All of this bring us in a roundabout way back to the deck of the Stubniz on that grey May morning watching Joon build an arcade cabinet out of borrowed equipment and supplies. It brings us to him and all the people who will play *LAZA KNITEZ!!* or *GO NUTS!!* over the next few days on this boat, to the community around these moments of DIY, to finding joy in the broken and the breaking , to trying even though you might fail completely, to supporting each other as we try, to just fucking doing it. That is what my DIY is, just fucking trying something. On balance I may have failed more than I've succeeded in these projects but I'm glad I throw myself at them with full gusto. Sleeping on floors, being broke, cardboard props are not what DIY is to me. DIY is about doing mad things with people that no else but you could do.

DO IT TOGETHER

I feel a little uncomfortable with the acronym DIY; and especially the notion of DIY in relation to the act of making theatre / performance. It's not the aesthetic that concerns me (in fact I quite like the low-tech, low-fi, low-budget look and feel of things). Instead, I have a problem with 'Doing It Yourself' as a politic of segregation.

Upon reflection, I have never been particularly good at 'doing it myself'. In fact, truth be told, I'm terrible at 'doing it myself'. It just doesn't work for me. The problem is, that to even suggest that I 'do it myself' makes me feel a fraud. Truth be told, I only ever manage to do anything much at all when I do it with the help of others. And these 'others' tend to be an extremely varied and atypical bunch. In the past, for example, I've been known to...

- Do It With Peers (DIWP)
- Do It With Friends (DIWF)
- Do It With Dramaturgs (DIWD)
- Do It With Provocateurs (DIWP)
- Do It With Strangers (DIWS)
- Do It With Supporters (DIWS)
- Do it With Students (DIWS)
- Do It With Directors (DIWD)
- Do It With Lighting Designers (DIWLD)
- Do It With Puppeteers (DIWP)
- Do It With Producers (DIWP)
- Do It With Musicians (DIWM)
- Do It With Professionals (DIWP)
- Do It With Dilettantes (DIWD)
- Do It With Funding Bodies (DIWFB)
- Do It With Foreigners (DIWF)
- Do It With Artists (DIWA)
- Do It With Parents (DIWP)

And the list continues beyond the limitations of these pages...

I've even been know to:
- Do It With Dead Artists Of The Past (DIWDAOTP)
- Do It With My Favourite Films (DIWMFF)

One time I even:
- Did It With A Children's Picture Book. (DIWACPB)

And the reason why I 'do it' with so many people and things is because the making of art is not (and has never been) a solipsistic act. To say that I 'Do It Myself' suggests an all too idealised autonomy; a suturing of myself from the communities within which I operate. For me, to 'Do It Myself' is a practical and philosophical impossibility. I am not capable of this hermetic essentialism even if I wanted to be. As John Donne famously states, 'no man [or woman] is an island'. We are all rich with influences, experiences and educations largely beyond our control or acknowledgement. And as such, I do not think, the phrase DIY (in relation to Theatre/Performance) is particularly indicative of the communities that it attempts to describe. It is a misnomer. It fails to do justice to the manifold opportunities and mutual cultures of support, coexistence, interconnectedness and influence that exists amongst independent artists. Very rarely, if at all, are we in positions where we are 'doing it ourselves'. Artist networks, resource sharing and ensemble practices are all paradigms that prove the interconnected, collectivist nature of our world. It is a rhizomatic network of goodwill, community and support that deserves celebrating and acknowledgement.

Art, after all, is never made in a vacuum; and it is dangerous to assume a position of autonomy outside of the world(s) within which we exist. The role of the artist is not, as I see it, to sit on the edge of culture and comment upon, as the anthropologist does, but instead (as the visual artist Joesph Kosuth suggests) to sit amongst cultures and peoples; shifting and manipulating them from within; as an 'anthropologist engaged'. The ethos of that ideal is predicated on the position that we must first, at least, acknowledge our interconnectedness; our sense of communitas.

In short, the act of 'Doing it Yourself' seems anathema to what I have witnessed to be the current interdependent practices inherent in the contemporary arts. Moreover, it just doesn't sit right with me. So instead I offer an alternative.

To DIW or to DIT... to 'Do It With' or even better, to...

DO IT TOGETHER

Reference
Kosuth, Joseph "Artist as Anthropologist" 1975 (extracts) reprinted in *The Everyday: Documents of Contemporary Art* edited by Stephen Johnstone. Cambridge, Mass. : MIT Press, 2008.

Childhood Pretenders

Recently I went for coffee with a childhood friend. I hadn't seen him in about five years, although we had been keeping up to date on each others lives through the power of Facebook. There was one thing that stayed with me from our three hour-long catch up as I drove back home on the A27. After the "hello, how are yous'", as soon as we sat down, he turned to me and said, "so I hear you make money now doing what we did as kids"

Nothing in his statement was false.

As children my friends and I played one game religiously from the age 9 onwards (this game was thrust upon me by my brother from and even earlier age) and even then this game probably lasted longer than it should have, and for me it hasn't stopped. It's a game we all played as children. We were pretenders.

We were pretenders and consumers. Every thing we witnessed (mainly TV & Film) had to be imitated and replicated in the best way possible. The best way possible when you're 9 is the use of everything around you. When you're 9 nothing is off limits: everything you use can and will have a use. Empty toilet roles were grenades, your garden was a jungle, the car park alley-way behind your house, with bumps and jumps, was the perfect setting for an all-out guns blazing bike/car chase. Soon we realised the local Tesco recycling bin was a cardboard haven (it still is) so now we could have backdrops and scenery!

Money and budgets have no meaning or purpose in pretending. We use what we find and we make it work. For me that's what's so special about DIY theatre. It perfectly taps into that childhood memory of pretending. When I see ripped up paper on an OHP being used to create city tower blocks or when someone sits me down in a chair, spins it around, and tells me I'm flying into space...im doing it! I don't care that the tennis balls on string have been painted into planets. If the paint's peeling and the tin foil's ripped, that only heightens the experience. Of course it's a taste thing, sometimes people need more and that's ok. We can always spot the real pretenders, the ones with a story to tell and only a tenner to make it happen. The real pretenders will go to great lengths to turn a hollowed out book and some card into a magical fairy tale. We like it because it takes us back to that childhood feeling of pretending.

I believe we are at our most creative when we have nothing but what we can find in the house. Anything is possible with enough gaffer tape!

My final thought is a task, a task for any artist or theatre maker whom might pick up this Book.

1. Find a friend.
2. Put aside one weekend.
3. Find as much cardboard as you can.
4. Decide on a shared favourite movie (hopefully this friend has similar movie interests) watch that movie on the Saturday morning.
5. Recreate that movie (with imaginary cameras) in the best way possible by Sunday evening.

I ask you to do this for one reason ... because its fun!

If you do find the time to do this, I would really love to hear about it. So please email Bootworks theatre. I'm sure our email is somewhere in this book.

Best ... Andy Roberts

1 Habits

I am at a stage of my career where it feels somehow fraudulent to claim to be writing about my process. Or perhaps I am just the kind of person who will always feel this way. Sometimes I am not sure I have 'a process'. But there are processes, of course. I make work. The way of doing so is no finite, circumscribable thing. It often follows rules, but they themselves are changeable. It makes no claim at authority or any guarantee of 'success'. It is, as yet, constantly 'in practice', learning itself, on a whim, often a frustration. But it is also not infinite, it gathers strength through the act of repetition, it may have a recognisable shape and rhythm, a 'set of inclinations, preoccupations' (to borrow from the introduction to this book). What I might feel more comfortable in thinking of as: 'habits'. And I fully acknowledge the implications of this word – of regularity, routine, norm, and therefore held within it the urge and necessity to also break these habits.

2 Process
- I begin, usually, with my own heartbreak.*
- I dream up or build a desire for the thing (work/piece/performance/show).
- I make the thing. (this sentence is misleadingly short)
- I try to come to terms with the thing that I have made.

3 DIY

If I had made a contribution to this book six years ago, when I first made collaborative work and used the phrase 'DIY' in relation to performance, it probably would have looked like a collage of images and scraps of text. I would have written about the use (and re-use) of everyday materials, a 'lo-fi' style, the beauty of 'showing how it's done'. I would at that time have articulated my understanding of 'DIY' as more about an aesthetic choice than about self-reliance and resourcefulness, but of course it was also driven by these things. Now I might say I try to make work in which an economy and flexibility are

inherent. Work that allows me to sustain the momentum of making and showing work, that allows me to embed a resilience into my practice, work that takes responsibility for itself. What I realise is that the 'DIY ethos' and I are in an ongoing and changing relationship. Both of us – like any good relationship – evolving, reinventing, and occasionally dolling ourselves up, for each other.

4 More thoughts on process & other bad habits
- The world is rich. The world is your clitoris, as my friend Anna used to say. Find things in it. Use found objects, images, texts, real people, fictional people, the internet, your own history and your future(s), the people you know, the people you want to know, research, youtube videos, music, sunlight. Imagination is your strongest tool and yet there is enough amazing truth in the world that you could get away without ever having to use your imagination at all.
- Trust your instincts and instinctual desires for a work, but try to avoid the belief that you should have infallible 'artistic instincts' and the pressure this will put you under. Your instincts are skills to be honed, informed always by experience, and also liable to be prejudiced or flawed.
- Be vulnerable. (A personal preference)
- Film yourself. Watch your footage with rigour. There might be one second of beauty within an hour. If you get bored, it is likely an audience will too.
- This is not my own thought, but one I am attached to (and can't remember where it came from): more often than not the information is less important than the attempt to communicate it.
- Like this page, within this book, context is powerful and rarely within your control.
- Make peace with your work. Practice coming to terms with the thing that you have made. I think this is worth repeating. You will likely have to do it every time.

5 Take a piece of A4 paper
Fold it lengthways down the middle. Make two lists:
- Words I would like people to use in describing
  my work.
- Words I would hate people to use in describing
  my work.

6 Heartbreak
* Heartbreaks might be of joy or fascination,
  a thought broken (open) by things vast and minute,
  whole ideologies or microscopic images. I don't
  mean, definitively, sadness, though there is often
  sadness at the core of the things that excite me.
  Sadness is alright.

do it, don't talk about it until you've done it, it is only become performance material when it has taken place in time & space, tailor to your circumstances, the problems presented are part of what makes the work, because it takes *place* in time & space those elements are incorporated, we took a trip to a tree which grew around a circle of displaced grave -stones, we made a crying machine, we played in the dirt, we took a long time, because we took so long we dreamed it and we didn't have

to feel as though we didn't know the piece yet, we had time to think about it, the *difference* between "thinking" and "making" is like the *difference* between the idea of a knife and the presence of the knife right here in my hand, accept the kind of thinking you can do on a full stomach, look both ways, a state of presence with each other can be fostered by a relaxed way of being together and holding open for possibilities and not straining to achieve but rather finding an active search, finding a way to put our bodies into it, we two found an even ground between us, throwing the body into action.

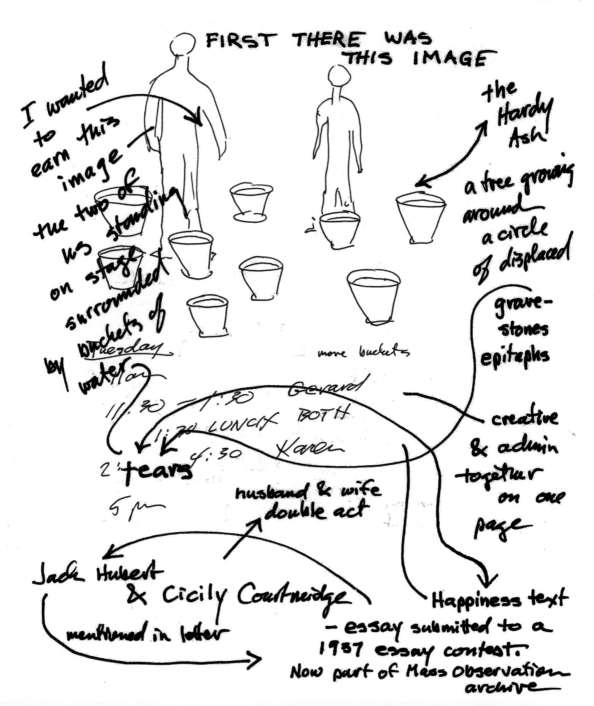

FIRST THERE WAS THIS IMAGE

I wanted to earn this image — the two of us standing on stage surrounded by buckets of Tuesday water

the Hardy Ash

a tree growing around a circle of displaced

grave-stones epitaphs

move buckets

creative & admin together on one page

11:30 → 1:30   Gerard
1:30 LUNCH   BOTH
4:30   Karen
2'tears
5 pm

husband & wife double act

Jack Hulbert & Cicily Courtneidge
mentioned in letter

Happiness text
— essay submitted to a 1957 essay contest. Now part of Mass Observation archive

{Watch this Sp a ce}

*"Our mind is the canvas upon which the
artists lay their colours, their pigments are
our emotions … the masterpiece is of
ourselves as we are of the masterpiece."* [i]
Kakuzo Okakura (1964)

Subject to_change is an art collective that aims to create live art works that are playful, immersive and transformative. It is committed to questioning the role of art in society by giving priority to audience engagement and their creative perception. Experience-led installations create temporary, dynamic and socially engaged communities. The installations invite audiences to collectively celebrate their individual contributions. Audiences become the artists, and in turn the 'artists' become facilitators. The durational installations create a space where over a period of time, the event shifts and changes in front of the audiences' eyes, and as the installation grows and transforms, so does their encounter with it. Audiences are encouraged to partake on a journey that is centered around a particular activity. This activity asks them to leave a trace of themselves in order for the artwork to live. I believe no other aesthetic would work. The content and deliberate choice of form are intrinsically linked.

The audience-centered experiences championed by Subject to_ change could be termed a 'DIY aesthetic'. Do It Yourself approach to work is rooted in non- professional, amateur work such as decorating or other home improvement work done without professional input. To translate this principle into an artistic context, it can be said that the participating audience member is a non-professional, whose involvement in the process of making charges them with agency and a responsibility for, if not the completion, then certainly an intrinsic contribution to the artwork. The audience members 'do it themselves', they make the work and physically build and change the landscape they are presented with. As well as providing a space where the roles of the artist and the spectator are interchangeable, DIY aesthetic can be an analogy extended to the materials that are made available in the artwork. Non- professional tools, objects and materials are used to make do and create an aesthetic that is both full of potential and at the same time, amateurish and imperfect. In this way the DIY aesthetic becomes a celebrated beauty in the art of imperfection it connotes – man-made and make-do.

This kind of philosophical approach and practical aesthetic characteristic of DIY can be seen in the works of Subject to_change. The coming together of the audience is vital for the installations to exist. The installations play with the imperfections of the 'amateur artist' by posing limitations where the work cannot become too slick or perfect. The use of everyday, craft materials and hobby activities creates a familiar playground that is carefully balanced within a professional framing, so that the worlds of the professional and non-professional can meet somewhere in the middle, mutually co-dependent yet teeming with potential. Tactile objects, physical actions, instructions and elements of risk are some of the tools that are used in crafting these DIY journeys. The environment participants come into has to be accessible, non- intimidating, a world of possibility and potential. It is my opinion that the use of DIY aesthetic is a way to create meaningful and interesting platforms for audiences to engage with.

The work that I, and Subject to_ change, make stems from a fascination in others. In the work a space is opened where the DIY aesthetic serves a literal and intellectual purpose. It is where questions of how art is made, to whom it is for and what separates the art (ist) from the view (er) are articulated and worked on. The Subject to_change works *home sweet home* (2006) and *Cupid* (2012) illustrate this point.

In *home sweet home* participants build their cardboard community over a period of time. They start with a flat packed miniature building and their chosen plot upon an outlined town on a canvas. The home-makers are provided with DIY tools to decorate their chosen building. Once this crafting of their home, or business, has finished, the participants begin to connect with neighbours through community devices such as the postal system, town councillor, local radio and notice board. The most compelling part of any home sweet home installation is the point where playful indignations trigger wider, more relevant, community issues and debates that are paralleled in the outside world. Due to its site-specificity each home sweet home community reflects and draws on its location and culture. From engaging with the DIY emblem of the flatpack to forging relationships with fellow non-professionals in their temporary roles as home-makers in these miniature communities, home sweet home keeps questioning how can performance open up playful and meaningful exchanges between both the artwork and the audiences that engage with it.

The performance installation *Cupid* is framed as an expedition - taking participants through the cosmos and into each other's hearts. The journey is broken by actions that are integral to the created environment(s) within the piece, where 'the doing of the action becomes a way of thinking about the image'[ii] itself. In the preparation room participants begin their journey by personalising their own white plaster heart. Next they are invited to meditate under a blanket of stars, and later asked to shoot with a real bow and arrow at another's heart that is suspended from the same cosmos under which they had previously laid. The installation is about making connections, shifting relationships and love. Ultimately its aim is to communicate the subtleties of mood and vagueness that compose the (non-) logic of the heart. Andy Field captures this saying, 'this is a dream landscape in which we can re-negotiate our relationship to the exhausted language of love'[iii]. Here again the materials of the work side by side the temporary relationships generate agency for the participants without which the work would not exist.

In other words, Subject to_ change installations aim to facilitate a space and time in which making and communicating are part of the process of engaging with the artwork. The commitment to the 'making of' bestows the audience with the power to take their time and space to create. The physical task given and/or the environment audiences walk into in Subject to_change installations become a personal platform for individual associations and memories to linger. In the words of the philosopher Gaston Bachelard all physical space holds a memory. It is 'thanks to the house, a great many of our memories are housed'.[iv] Subject to_ change use familiar or iconic environments to encourage individual's memories to be unpacked. The audience member's 'head space' becomes part of the performance by giving space and time to an activity that allows thoughts and actions to mingle and co-exist in the same space. As the objects and images change, so does the content and perspective.

DIY approaches to theatre and live art making create a holistic space. It can be considered as a physical and mental space to think, to explore, to learn and to play. It is a where words and images are not shouted, dictated or autocratic but where they embrace their own invention.

It is a where chance events invite physical and/or mental participation, which build creative tension. This space is an exciting space to be in because 'When the image is new, the world is new'.[v] The space where art and life can meet is where new theatre exists.

The Japanese have a word Ma (間) that interpreted means space-time. Ma is not a blank space within which nothing moves. Silence is only recognised as silence when sound is dropped into the void. Japanese architecture, gardening, painting, stories, tea ceremonies or poetry act as a necessary vehicle to 'experience' this void. Ma is a relational entity where space is divided invisibly by ones own breath and movements. One moves through time in a constant circumbulation of potential transformation, 'a never ending state of becoming and dissolving.'[vi] This can be seen at the very core of Japanese art and culture but I think it also resonates deeply for DIY approaches to live art and theatre making.

'True beauty could be discovered only by one who mentally completed the incomplete…it is left for each guest in imagination to complete the total effect in relation to himself'.[vii]

I will now hand this over to you, the participant, The Masterpiece.

Taking my inspiration from the Chinese one corner paintings which reflect the need to experience a space where the mind can complete the picture I leave you with a torch and a 'blank page with the 'right to dream'.[vii]

Use the next page to ask yourself a question. What do you see illuminated in the void?

And as an afterthought, no matter how small, keep some space for others to drop things into the void too.

Watch This Space!

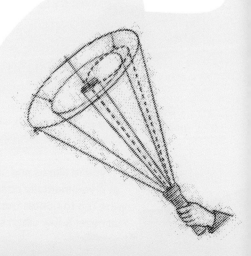

Bibliography

- Bachelard, G. (1969) *The Poetics of space*, Beacon press: Boston.
- Bachelard, G. (1969) *The Poetics of Reverie*, Orion Press: New York
- Field, A. *Cupid review*. This is tomorrow online.
  http://www.thisistomorrow.info/viewArticle.aspx?artId=1221 1 April 2012
- Koren. L. (1994) *Wabi- Sabi. For Artists Designers, Poets and Philosophers*,
  Published by Stone Bridge Press, Berkely, California USA
- Okakura. K. (1964) *The Book of Tea*, Dover Publications, Inc. New York
- Shimmel. (1998) *Tracing Live Art- Performance From Actions To The Body*

References

[i] Okakura. Kakuzo *The Book of Tea*. (New York: Dover Publications.1964), P.78
[ii] Field, Andy. '*This is tomorrow*'. Online.
http://www.thisistomorrow.info/viewArticle.aspx?artId=1221 1 April 2012
[iii] Ibid.
[iv] Bachelard, Gaston. *The Poetics of space*, (Boston: Beacon press.1969), P.8
[v] Bachelard, Gaston. *The Poetics of space*, (Boston: Beacon press. 1969). P.47
[vi] Koren. Leonard. *Wabi- Sabi. For Artists Designers, Poets and Philosophers*.
  (Berkeley: Stone Bridge Press, 1994), P.49
[vii] Okakura. Kakuzo *The Book of Tea*. (New York: Dover Publications.1964). P.70
[viii] Bachelard, Gaston. *The Poetics of Reverie*. (New York: Orion Press.1969). P.17

COOL HUNTING

From Beginners to Beginners...

Hello. We're Daniel + Rachel. As a new company currently exploring a D.I.Y Work ethic and still finding our feet, we wondered what we had to offer when asked to contribute to this book. The answer: a beginner's insight.

What now follows are five little Pointers that have been helpful for us as a company in our early days. We hope you find them as useful as we have.

TAKE EVERY OPPORTUNITY.

Talk to everyone and anyone – you never know what will come from a conversation, a short e-mail, or even a passing comment.

Creating a twitter, facebook or youtube account can go a long way when starting out. The majority of the people you want to connect to are online. Think of who your heroes are and follow them on these sites, see what they're doing and maybe even try to start an online dialogue.

ONE MANS TRASH IS ANOTHER MANS TREASURE.

Don't be afraid to explore recycling bins. They can be gold mines when you're strapped for cash.

It's okay to be a hoarder – If you're like us and like to keep everything from receipts to old birthday cards, or if you mentally hoard from remembering lines to a song you heard when you were ten to quotes from a film you can't remember the name of, be proud of this. You never know when such seemingly useless objects and information will come in handy.

THE AUDIENCE ARE YOUR FRIENDS.

Imagine you are five years old again and are playing a game of pretend with your friends. You only have a sandpit, a tea set and some crayons, but you are adamant that today you are going to be spaceman. To do this, you need to convince your friends that what you have can be used as moon rocks, walkie talkies, and comets. In this case, your audience are your childhood friends.

With this in mind, don't exclude your friends – DIY theatre, with it's rough and relaxed attitude opens eyes to an exciting and creative form that belongs to nobody, a form performed for everyone and created for all.

IF IT'S NOT WORKING IT'S STILL WORTH IT.

Don't be afraid to kill your babies (metaphorically speaking, of course) – be brutal and more importantly be realistic. If it doesn't aid the piece anymore, get rid of it, be open to change and move on. From what we've learnt recently both from others and ourselves, performances suffer if you can't let go of your initial ideas.

If you're really not ready to let go, put a pin in it and come back to it another time

START A RIOT!

It is important to remember that what you're doing when applying a DIY attitude is a subtle form of protest.

DIY is an alternative that allows us to gain back the authority of our own work and benefit anyone who experiences it.

It is a way of working born out of a drive to imagine the unimaginable, create the uncreatable and turn fantasies into realities using what little resources there are to do so.

The REDUX

Richard DeDomenici

So I guess it all started in April 2009 when I was on my way by train to Hamburg to attend the Aircraft Interiors Expo. I had some spare time at Gare De L'Est station in Paris, so decided to attempt to remake a section of the film *Amelie* (Jeunet, 2001) which had been filmed on the steps outside. This was hampered by my sub-GCSE French, and the fact that I hadn't seen the film for several years.

Two years later, at Berlin's Ostbahnhof station, I recognised a location from one of the Bourne films. By now I had embraced the smartphone revolution, and so was able to find the clip on YouTube, and make a shot-for-shot remake of what is admittedly the most boring 60 seconds of *The Bourne Supremacy* (Greengrass, 2004). At home I edited the footage together using a fancy new bit of editing software. I was able to place the original footage alongside my own, and colour grade it in such a way as it looked quite similar.

This was not yet a conscious art project, merely something to occupy my time whilst waiting at foreign train stations. However, when Forest Fringe asked me in 2012 if I had any ideas for a project at the Scala Cinema in Bangkok, I decided to revisit this shot-for-shot/original location methodology. And so it was that in early 2013 I remade six minutes of the highest grossing movie in Thailand in 2009: *Bangkok Traffic Love Story* (Tresirikasem).

I made the last-minute decision to play the lead, and the rest of the cast and crew were recruited locally. When we weren't filming I was busy editing, and we showed daily rushes in a production office at the cinema. It was very ambitious to find the locations, shoot and edit the footage in four days, although we saved time by filming without permission, which meant we often only had a single take. On the final night of the festival, and with minutes to spare, we screened the finished edit at The Scala. Wise Kwai, film critic for The Nation newspaper, wrote that he liked our version more than the original. Enthused, me and colleagues Andy Field and Brian Lobel filmed a scene from the groundbreaking romantic drama *The Love of Siam* (Sakveerakul, 2007), before we left.

The Nation's critic wrote: 'It's not near as complicated as the remake of Bangkok Traffic Love Story, but is perhaps even more valuable as a homage to one of Thai cinema's great moments inside Bangkok's last remaining single-screen movie theater.' Then, to our surprise, *The Love Of Siam's* Director Chookiat Sakveerakul posted our version on his Facebook page. So I'd like to thank the people of Bangkok for being so understanding, and for tolerating the most unconvincing ladyboy in Thailand. I calculated that were I to make the rest of *Bangkok Traffic Love Story* it would take two months and cost £14,000, but unfortunately the British Council have yet to make this happen. Back in the United Kingdom, I showed my series of remakes – now collectively referred to as *The Redux Project* – as part of my touring show *Popaganda*.

I explained in *Popaganda* that the project was a comment on, and contribution to, the increasingly derivative nature of mainstream cinema; how It's rare to see a Hollywood film these days that isn't a sequel, remake, or adaptation; that the Bourne films are a combination of all these; and that the word Redux means 'brought back', and is a term I stole from Francis Ford Coppola. I went onto to posit that *The Redux Project* was my attempt to disrupt the studio system by making counterfeit versions of popular movies. One night, on the train back from a gig in Brighton, I met two audience members, Caroline and Alex, who told me they were about to travel to Goa, where some of *The Bourne Supremacy* was filmed. It was at this point that I decided to make The Redux Project open-source. I sent Caroline and Alex an extremely detailed shot list, and essentially ruined their holiday by making them spend all their time remaking bits of Bourne. I edited the footage they bought back, resulting in an additional 38 seconds of the trilogy. But there's still another 343 mins to go, and I can't possibly visit all the locations myself, so if anyone reading this is going to Madrid, Moscow, Mykonos, New York, Paris, Prague, Rome, Tangier or Zurich, do get in touch.

We can make it together. It'll be beautiful.

Admittedly I'll get most of the credit, but then that's the nature of participatory art. With Bangkok as a successful proof-of-concept, I decided to attempt another Redux. To reduce costs, several of the scenes from *Cloud Atlas* (Wachowski/Twyker, 2012) set in 1973 San Francisco were actually filmed in Glasgow. I noticed this because many were filmed along the route I used to walk to the Arches when I used to perform at the National Review of Live Art, albeit heavily augmented with CGI to look more Californian. Buildings were replaced, and telegraph poles added, in quite a convincing way, although there are some clues that we're not in 1973 San Francisco, most notably an accessibility elevator, which were rarities at the time, and tactile paving, which has only been mandatory in California since 2001.

It was these two and a half minutes of 1973 San Francisco street scenes that we remade over 48 hours at the Buzzcut Festival in March 2013. It was the most ambitious Redux yet, involving multiple actors, stunts, props, guns, car crashes, broken glass, and freezing winds.

I screened the finished edit at the end of Buzzcut, and a reviewer from The Scotsman gave it a four star review: *"Richard Dedomenici's outrageous reworking of Cloud Atlas is hilarious but also piercing, a sharp critique of modern myth-making and fierce in identifying the lies that buttress existing power, and threaten to make fools of us all."* ****

So even though The Redux project by its very nature creates derivative work. Which, in doing so, would contradict the first law of thermodynamics. If you want to try and get a five-star review from The Scotsman, try making a remake of my remake of *Cloud Atlas*, and let me know what happens. This summer as part of my Edinburgh Fringe run of *Popaganda* I remade sections of the romantic drama *One Day* (Scherfig, 2011).

And learned a valuable lesson that if you make a Redux shot too perfect, people won't believe that it's a Redux.

I had to flip the title to curb accusations that I'd lifted it from the original. We quickly got bored of remaking *One Day* and so decided to Redux the kitchen scene from Jurassic Park (Spielberg, 1993) instead.

I know what you're thinking, *Jurassic Park* wasn't filmed in Edinburgh. Well occasionally I relax the Redux rules, like that night I reshot the opening titles of *Hawaii Five-O* in the Hunt & Darton Cafe in Clapton.

My most recent Redux, *Dawn Of The Dead* (Romero, 1978), also flagrantly broke the site-specific stipulation by not being shot in an empty shopping centre near Pittsburgh, but an empty shopping centre in Kendal.

Frankly I was so excited to have free reign of an empty shopping centre, and thirty zombie extras in full make-up, that I was willing to overlook this.

So, less than a year into the project, and I'm already watering down one of the few key principles of *The Redux Project* that make it unique.

Forthcoming Reduxes include *The Duchess* (Dibb, 2008) at the Bath Fringe, *The Bourne Ultimatum* (Greengrass, 2007) with the National Theatre Studios in Waterloo, *Fallen Angels* (Kar Wai, 1995) in Hong Kong, *Pricilla: Queen of the Desert* (Elliot, 1994), *Murial's Wedding* (Hogan, 1994), *Mad Max Beyond Thunderdome* (Millar, 1985) and *The Matrix* (Wachowski, 1999) at the Sydney Festival, and if I'm very lucky *Superman IV: The Quest For Peace* (Furie, 1987) in Milton Keynes.

I always used to criticise artists who only have one idea, then repeat that idea around the world in perpetuity until they run out of venues. But maybe I was just jealous. I guess It's ok so long as its a good idea.

While I'm not sure if *The Redux Project* is great art, I'll continue the franchise until I get bored, or Hollywood sues, whichever happens faster. Because I hope that, by making a fake version of something that is already fake, we can somehow eventually arrive at the truth.

Watch all the Reduxes and get involved at www.TheReduxProject.com, for any other business, visit www.DeDomenici.com

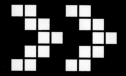

Dirty Market, Roughing up the Classics game.

"I don't like theatre, but I like this!"
Audience member after DMT's Yerma Rough
Classics Workshop.

We've always defined ourselves as DIY - out of necessity
at first, then as an aesthetic choice - our shows definitely
have a homemade feel to them.

'Dirty Market' - the nickname for a big junk market
Georgina grew up close to in Scotland, where the flotsam
and jetsam of people's lives washed up. A trip to the Dirty
Market meant entering an alternative world, stumbling
through piles of clothes and furniture, discovering
oddities... and sometimes treasure. You'd step in and out
of imagined stories, the detritus of people's lives piled
together randomly, creating new narratives.

There's another market, in Varanasi, India, where
mountains of discarded electronic goods are taken apart
and sorted into piles and then expertly rebuilt into 'new'
items by tinkerers, craftsman - bricoleurs.

DIY is not just about making theatre on the cheap (though
it can be a lot cheaper). With DIY theatre you get the
opportunity to harness everyone's creative energies,
getting the best answers from surprising places - (What?
Actors have ideas worth listening to? My God! The Stage
Manager is sitting silently on the answer to my thorny
problem? Ouch...).

Sometimes it's a bit chaotic and the answers don't come
as quickly as usual when employing those tried-and-tested
"well-made play" methodologies. But those
old methods usually guarantee a certain sameness,
a one-size-fits-all theatre.

The audience gets the theatre they expect, which
is fine of course.

But throwing away the old rule book creates space.
And that's space for more than just new work. It has
the potential to be a place where new healthier attitudes
towards each other can take root, where everyone -
audience included - can uncover and develop new abilities
and talents, and where everyone has the opportunity to
become one of the 'creatives'.

THE ROUGH CLASSICS GAME

Jon was initially introduced to task-based performance
with instructions laid out on a pack of cards, during
a workshop led by DV8's Wendy Houston. In fact, we still
use some of the task cards from her original 'deck'. Over
the years though, we have adapted the exercise to fit our
practice of pulling apart, creating out of and rebuilding
extant texts. Our Rough Classics workshops now
culminate in a public task-card game, but we also use
this game as a tool for exploring and combining material
when devising.

We break the text down into small parts, and then the
group create tiny performances out of each part,
transforming the original through the filter of their
imagination and life experience. These become
components in the game which in turn, will piece them
together in random, surprising ways.
We start to discover as a group, the elements that feel
important - what is to be foregrounded...

Rami Nasr, a regular workshopper, told us recently that
the process of extracting themes from the source text,
distilling them into actions to be played again and again
in random ways, gives the performer a direct and
embodied experience of more abstract ideas and helps
build a firmer understanding.

Pulling the ideas out and then 'shuffling the deck' breaks
the narrative stranglehold of the piece and offers new
ways to connect with the ideas / themes / actions.

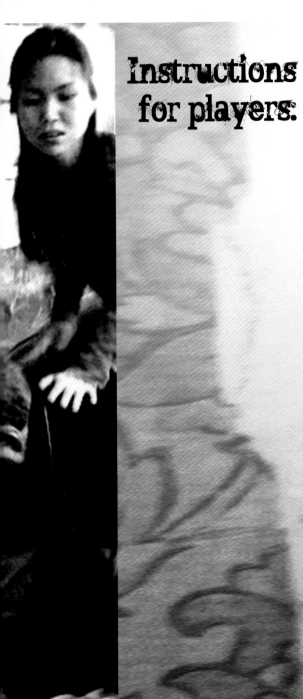

Instructions for players.

ONE - GATHERING MATERIAL
- To prepare for the game we collect / make an assortment of performance responses to the text. These include: individually devised short responses - inspired by the 'impossible tasks' of Goat Island, free writes, early character work (gestural, expressive, hot seat material etc...), short compositions.
- We browse the text and pull out key actions, themes, striking images, seemingly inconsequential moments.
- Then, like seasoning, we add an assortment of more generic composition elements (Anne Bogart's Viewpoints are useful for this).

TWO - PREPARATION
- All the instructions are written on separate cards and the deck shuffled and placed in a prominent position between the audience and playing space.
- Sometimes we mark with tape particular areas of the performance space, for example, the monologue box or the scene box, to give the space some rules, cohesion or conditions of play.
- Certain tasks can also have time limits and for this we use an egg timer.

THREE - PLAY
- Players are also the audience and sit facing the action.
- When they feel the urge, players take a card from the top of the pack, read it and place it to the bottom (NB: if the game is a public event - we found it helps if the non-playing audience have an opportunity to see the task somehow before it is replaced in the pack).
- Players are not obliged to perform the task immediately.
- Once they have performed their task, players return to their seats, draw another card and watch and wait for the right time to return to the action.

QUESTIONS FOR THE PLAYERS
- Where in the space should you perform the task?
- Do you want to compliment or contrast the existing action?
- Think of the durational choices - for how long are you going to perform the task?
- Do you want to play it loud or soft / slow or fast / in what style / attitude / emotion?
- Do you want to add to the existing action, or take the action somewhere else?
- A sudden change, or a gradual one?
- How to get into the space?
- Is the stage too busy? Are all the layers connected?

GENERAL NOTES TO PLAYERS
- This is not a directed exercise - there is no one in charge - you are in charge! Let the action in the space inspire your next move.
- Remember to watch / observe / listen..
- ...and in performing, to react and respond.
- This is a rehearsal exercise - its a non-hierarchical exploration - no one should tell you what to do!

An improvised music score can help things along in terms of mood and atmosphere, as, if facilities permit, can a few changes in lighting. These jobs could be added as task cards if all present are playing.

EXAMPLE TASK LISTS
The following list was compiled during the early rehearsal stages of Something About You (makes me want to hurt you) our adaptation of Euripides' Electra. We had a public work-in-progress showing of the task game which we called, Electraloop.

- Mirror someone
- Point to the action
- Destroy something - then describe what you've created
- Move the knife
- Support someone
- Sing a lullaby
- Antagonise someone
- Change the space
- Dance for the gods
- 3 x Speak a line from your chosen text (research texts including articles on children who kill)
- Hide in the space
- Walk into darkness
- Balance the space
- Die slowly
- Applaud the action
- Start an argument
- Put on high heels and walk like Electra (previously devised short score)
- Read through the task list quietly
- Hang up washing (previously devised short score)
- Change your sex
- 3 x Perform a character loop (including gestures, floor patterns and actions)
- Ask a question to which the answer is Electra
- Be a mirror
- Play the shipping forecast
- 3 x Perform an element from the character loops

- 3 x Go to the text box - speak for 2 minutes... on mothers / fathers / families
- Be Clytemnestra - wait for Electra
- Be Electra - wait for Clytemnestra
- Play a scene
- Fetch water
- Cut your hair
- Make an offering
- Lament
- Recognise someone
- Betray someone
- Make a loud noise
- Passionately kiss someone
- Wait
- Count to ten
- Cross the space - slow tempo
- Perform an action / gesture in ultra slow motion
- Perform a floor pattern at an slow or fast tempo
- Break an egg
- Plead for your life
- 3 x Perform your solo short score
- Echo someone
- Repeat a gesture 15 times at ultra fast tempo
- Laugh incessantly
- 2 x Do an expressive gesture - centre stage
- Watch someone
- Be a dog
- Say what you think
- Narrate what you see happening
- Tell a true secret
- Perform a pause
- Hug someone
- Describe what you understand by home
- Repeat a character gesture 15 times
- Perform an action very slowly
- Perform an action very fast
- Call the company to follow you in a choral dance
- Call the company to follow someone in a choral dance
- 3 x Describe what you understand by 'presence' / 'identity' / 'role'

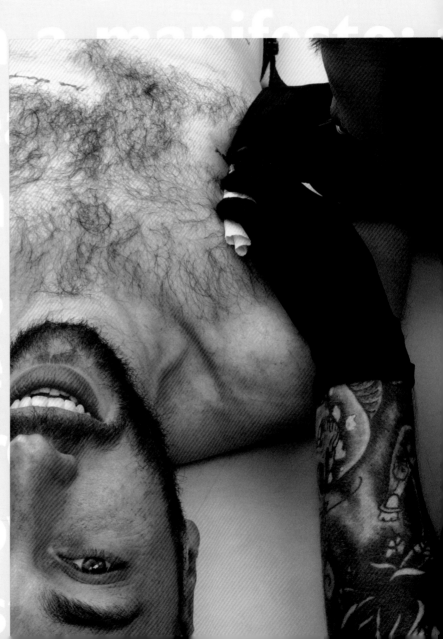

nd, to find ou
ve recently be
on. whatever),
along
docu
ve ju

ought we wou
a manifesto

not hoi
t resi

HOBBYISTS

. . . .

the fictional dogshelf theatre company
Joanne 'Bob' Whalley & Lee Miller

We had thought we would begin with a manifesto: a simple, clear call to arms of resistance. Resisting the corporate, the showy, the skilful, the valued. But this isn't really very 'us'. It's not how we work. We don't resist the tropes of large-scale performance making in any particularly mindful way, rather we do what we are interested in with the materials we have to hand. Perhaps that is why we have spent twenty years working together: we've both been the closest person to hand. As might be expected, an easy shorthand has developed between us in this time, and perhaps our fondness for working with each other comes as much from laziness as from anything else. We don't think that is the case, but even if it was, it wouldn't matter too much.

Perhaps we are getting ahead of ourselves. By starting with a defence of what we haven't done, we're missing the obvious. So, pretend you didn't read the first paragraph, pretend we're only just starting now... We are here by accident.

Obviously, not a complete accident, I mean we it's not as if we tripped over and fell on the keyboard, the words you read are the result of conversation and debate, they are not simply the artefact of our fingers hitting random buttons as we try to right ourselves once more. The accident to which we refer happened some time ago. Of course its age does not make it any less accidental. So perhaps we should shift out of the confessional and into the contextual. Our story begins with an accident, nothing cataclysmic, simply the wrong glance cast out of the wrong window at the wrong moment.

We met in 1992, married in 1996, got a dog the same year, moved across the country, and lived in two large cities, one small city, one remote cottage, a village in Cheshire, an unremarkable town in the east Midlands and now in a house behind a shop, a house that no one can ever find in a town on a hill in Devon. Altogether, nine different houses and flats. Somewhere in that jumble of houses one dog died and another one joined us, with an overlap of four years which was filled with barking and attendant behavioural issues.

As one might expect, the nineteen year olds who met back then had no particular plan, no roadmap indicating where they might be headed. Various jobs were held, a fairly typical litany of arts graduate employment; retail, catering, working in a hotel, becoming an apprentice potter, answering the phones in call centres, cleaning toilets and selling pornography and cigarettes to truck drivers. No rhyme, no reason. Certainly there was no plan, and no hint at the development of an emerging performance art practice.

Which is, after all, what we've been charged to write about. During the course of our relationship, there have been points where one of us has needed to live away from home, and it was during one of these brief periods that our approach to making performance work really began. The way we work has its origins in the chance observation of what appeared to be a bottle of urine, lying abandoned on the hard shoulder of the M6 motorway. In order to confirm our suspicions, we stopped to collect it, and having seen one bottle, we began to see them at regular intervals along the hard shoulder. Knowing that these bottles and their contents were the product of fellow travellers, Bob felt uncomfortable about simply taking them, and so it was decided that we needed to make some sort of exchange. At first we left behind whatever we had in our pockets (coins, tissues, paid utility bills), but this developed into keeping a

selection of items in the car, gifts that had been given to us, things with some provenance, things we could exchange for the bottles of urine we found on our travels. We were both in the car; one of us made the observation, the other made the exchange. It was in that moment that our approach to making performance practice really began, although we certainly could not have articulated in this way at the time.

We had been working together before this. We had collaborated on projects during our degree course, and following that toured theatre into schools, eventually setting up our own company, which focussed primarily upon taking theatre into rural schools. In all of this, we were still serving the needs of others: whether they were playwrights, teachers or the national curriculum, our making was focussed upon delivering something according to other people's needs.

The bottles of piss changed this. For us, rather than functioning as detritus, the bottles of piss became an invitation of sorts. We spent the next two years thinking and experimenting (when you have been together a long time, you can move at a more glacial speed), and eventually, on Friday 20th September 2002 we invited fifty family, friends and interested parties to the Roadchef Sandbach Services between junctions 16 and 17 of the M6 for the performance event *Partly Cloudy, Chance of Rain*. Between the hours of 11 am and 4 pm, the site was occupied by ten performers in wedding dresses, ten performers in morning suits, a six strong choir, a three-piece jazz-funk band, a keyboard player and a priest. At twelve thirty, we renewed our wedding vows in a ceremony that was open to all the users of the service station. After the ceremony, our guests were taken on a guided tour of the site, and users of the service station were witness to a variety of performance actions.

Everything we have done from that point has begun from the things we find close at hand, and the conversations we have at the dinner table, in front of the TV or in bed.

We sometimes call our accidents 'Beginnings With Our Eyes Shut' as this seems to us to be a good place to start. We like to 'bimble' (you might find this hard to believe, but this is a technical term: Edward Casey celebrates the cultural practice of 'bimbling'), to go for a wander with our ideas, find the other routes, the other possibilities to our practice: to explore where the dangers are and chart the unexplored lands.

You will, of course, be very familiar with phosphenes, even though you might not know their name. Phosphenes are the whorls of colour and light that you see on the inside of your eyelids as you prepare for slumber. They are the residual retinal images, the perception of light without actual light that will eventually transform into full-blown dreams. And that is where we start our practice, eyes wide shut, watching our own eyelids. Watching as the visual snow swirls around, waiting

for something, anything to come into focus. We are told that there is currently no established treatment for this snow we suffer from, that it is a transitory symptom, and that we should wait, as all will soon become clear. Our forays into making performance feel to us a little like waiting to fall asleep; things start to form — shapes as yet unknown furring up the edges of our vision, wait just outside of our reach. And this is, of course, frustrating. We want to know now, want to see what all the possibilities are, know what the plans are and where we sit within them. But this frustration is like the snow, something that comes with the territory, something that will soon pass. So we just lie there, and dream long term.

Someone once told us that if you have a strong opening and a solid finish, the audience will forgive you the middle. When engaged in our own performance practice it is probably safe to say that we have fallen into the habit of focussing on the beginning. Truth be told, we quite like starting things. Introductions tend to make us smile. Letting you know who we are, what to expect and what your role will be. Perhaps those amateur psychologists among you have some comments to make about the individual that clings doggedly to beginnings. Perhaps you feel that is says something telling about our ability to commit, or perhaps indicates lack of staying power. And perhaps those amateur psychologists might be correct; beginnings are easy. They're full of grand gestures and winks at the camera. They're all about pulling you in, inviting, enticing. Making you welcome. We can do beginnings with our eyes shut. We have a great track record with beginnings. We've started more things than it is possible to finish.

And yet...
There is something unsettling about beginnings, like the snow behind our eyelids, the phosphenes that find us in the dark — they speak of many things. Once beginnings are done and dusted that is

where the really hard work happens, because soon you have sailed out of the beginning, and you are somewhere in the middle; that big stretch that is so difficult to fill. The middle is the thing our friend said you will be forgiven for if you start well and end with a flourish. But what might be true of performance is never true in life. The middle is quite possibly the thing that defines you, that allows people to understand the context in which you function. And it is the middle that we find ourselves contemplating, as we try to define what it is that we do.

As a result of that initial discovery, that accidental stumbling across a discarded bottle, all of our subsequent practice has inhabited spaces that tend to be transactional in some way — that is to say, they are rarely spaces of dwelling, never home in the most traditional sense. Perhaps we are obsessed with journeys, with the things in between A and B simply because we are not well travelled. Well travelled suggests a certain glamour, a movement, a freedom where the world is something with which you are intimately familiar. To us, it speaks of a sophistication that does not sit well in our bodies. Of course, that sophistication might not be a Madison Avenue martini kind of a thing; it might be an Ashram in India, or a Yurt in Mongolia, that sort of thing. Whatever, it's not something we have. Sadly, we don't do sophisticated. We don't do at ease. We do gauche, we do awkward and we do them very well. No, we are not well travelled. But there are 104,000 miles on the clock of our current car, and we hit 24,000 miles on our last one, 24,000 miles for the second time. No, we aren't well travelled, but we are much travelled.

We've spent the majority of the past 21 years looking out of various windows, at varying landscapes as they blur by. The much-travelled individual probably doesn't engage in the voyage of discovery. Their travels are unlikely to be the kinds that lead to some sort of edification. They are much more likely to be the kind of journey that ends on a stranger's doorstep with a Kirby™ vacuum cleaner or something in tow, and a hopeful smile on their face. And we are sitting here, stationary in front of our keyboards, still but thinking about movement, and suddenly we feel shy about our bimbling as, looking at the clock (we've both just past forty), it indicates that we are steaming out of the middle and if the middle is what defines us then there may be some difficulties here as we hurtle towards the end.

As we try to come to some sort of.... well, if not conclusion, some sort of temporary triage that might stitch up our wounded thoughts, as we try to think about what exactly it is that we are offering, if it is not a manifesto, we think we might have found a way in: a term that might hold the accidental aesthetic that has ghosted our practice. We've decided that we quite like epithet 'hobbyist'; it seems a comfortable fit. This is perhaps because whilst skill, experience and knowledge are all our part of our avocational mantra, glory is not. In fact, it may come as a surprise to you, but we're not in this for the fame or the money. As a result, 'Hobbyist' has become something of a golden word to us, but this does not mean that we are shoddy in our undertaking. We are indeed wilful Dilettantes, dabblers even, but we do not treat our engagement with our making practices in a superficial way. It is not entirely uncommon for a hobbyist to be the first to discover something that no one else has seen or heard or thought of before. To ride one's hobbyhorse, is of course, a very personal affair, and the aim of the hobbyist is not necessarily for the gains that are to be made, rather it is for personal fulfilment, for the joy of the thing.

And perhaps this realisation, this settling on nomenclature is more than just a confession. Maybe it is our attempt to define a margin, to articulate critically our understanding (or lack thereof) of

what we do. And it is at this point, at the moment where we confess this to ourselves, where we recognise that our work comes from the wrong end of the day, from the bottle discarded on along the hard shoulder, from the wilful misunderstanding of invitations made to us.

But maybe this is no bad thing. Perhaps our claimed status of hobbyist is actually a transgression; are we seeding subtle radicalism when we suggest that we can't be considered professional, not really, not when our bills are paid by doing things like teaching and admin, rather than doing things like performing in a motorway service station, a shopping mall or an abandoned city centre bathroom shop. Our practice is deliberately diffuse, described recently by a curator of a gallery we worked with as 'promiscuous', suggesting that we will go anywhere with anyone. Certainly 'promiscuous' appeals to us as a description much more than 'unfocussed'.

One thing that we are aware of is the fact that throughout our bimbling, the domestic has always featured heavily in our work. Home has always been that unspoken other, that ghost in the machine that tries to quietly assert itself. Perhaps it comes as no surprise that as we cast about for the next thing, we keep returning to our kitchen table, to cooking for and talking with our audience. But maybe they aren't an audience, maybe we can start to say 'there's no such thing as an audience, only friends you haven't met yet'.

And maybe this might translate into something showy, something large scale, something like our long-imagined but never realised piece Home for the Holidays. We picture ourselves renting a shop in Manchester Airport for all of December, of putting up those hoardings that prevent people looking in. We imagine lots of to-ing and fro-ing, men and women carrying hods and plasterboard, lengths of 3" x 2". We imagine a radio tuned to Radio

One... ALL DAY. Then, after a week or two, certainly well in advance of Christmas Eve, the hoardings would come down, and the shop would look like our front room. Or at least it might look something like it. And then we would go about our business, we would write out cards, we would wrap up presents, we would argue about whose family we could get away without visiting. We'd have friends over, we'd watch Sky and sing along to the carols they play on the menu screen. We'd walk about in our underpants. Well, I'd walk about in my underpants. And then we'd go out for walks. We'd look for people who had missed their connection, for people who were needing a break, for people who were all finding it a bit too much. And then we'd have them over for tea. We'd give them mince pies; we'd try to cheer them up by letting them play with our dog. And on Christmas Day, we'd let them all sit around the tree and open presents.

At least, that's the plan. But once we're there and people have had their pies, we're not quite sure what would come next.

Perhaps this is because we have always wanted to take you with us on a tour of all our favourite places. The places between A and B, the places that you would probably like to forget. Only we can't take you with us, not really. You wouldn't all fit in the car, and even if you could, there would be arguments about which junction to take, who's riding shotgun, and where is the best place to park.

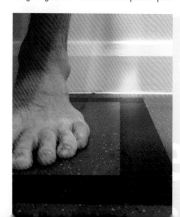

14 WAYS TO TURN THIS BOOK INTO A PERFORMANCE

1. Choose a page at random. Read aloud in a situation provided with maximum amplification.

2. Choose a page at random and memorise it. Recite it silently in your head as you walk:
   - Along a crowded street
   - Down a country road
   - To a meeting you are dreading
   - Around a room you are not supposed to be in

3. Choose a sentence at random and cut it out of the book with scissors or a sharp knife. Fold it up and hand it to a stranger next time you are at the theatre.

4. On the book
     a grater
     tape measure
     alphabet
     flag

     black
             and spectral colors

5. Choose an artist from this book at random. Imagine them:
   - Washing stains out of an old uniform
   - Sitting in a car flicking the headlights on and off and on and off
   - Throwing powder paint into a swimming pool
   - Replying to emails
   - Kissing someone inappropriate

6. Choose a page at random and tear it out of the book. Find a large Tupperware container and fill it completely with water. Place the page into the Tupperware container and hold it there until it sinks. Place the Tupperware container in a freezer. Wait. Remove the Tupperware container from the freezer and remove the block of ice from the Tupperware container. Begin walking, carrying the block of ice. Walk towards the nearest town centre, or along the side of a ring road, or follow a desire line across a field. Keep walking until the ice has completely melted and you are left with only the page of this book that was frozen inside it. Stop. Notice where you have stopped. Leave the page from the book in this spot, perhaps pinned to a tree or slipped behind the windscreen wiper of a parked car.

7. Take the book to a café. Pretend to be reading the book but do not actually read the book. Use any of the following actions:
   - Gentle nod of head
   - Confused frown
   - Lick finger and turn page
   - Look up from book and stare briefly into distance
   - Blink too much
   - Fold corner of page
   - Smile fondly

8. Choose your favourite page in the book. Remember which page it is.

9. Balance the book on a table or the floor, spine up so that it looks like a chapel or a church. Think about the people in the church and how they are all singing together and how loudly they are all singing.

10. Cut every page of the book into very small squares. Use these squares:
    - as confetti at an imaginary wedding
    - as snow in an imaginary winter
    - as stars in an imaginary universe
    - to spell out a message on beach
    - as fragments of an entirely different book awaiting reassembly

11. Read a shopping list or the classified ads in a newspaper with the concentration you have been giving to this book.

12. Use this book to set something on fire.

13. Use this book to set everything on fire.

14. Trade this book for a ticket to the opera.

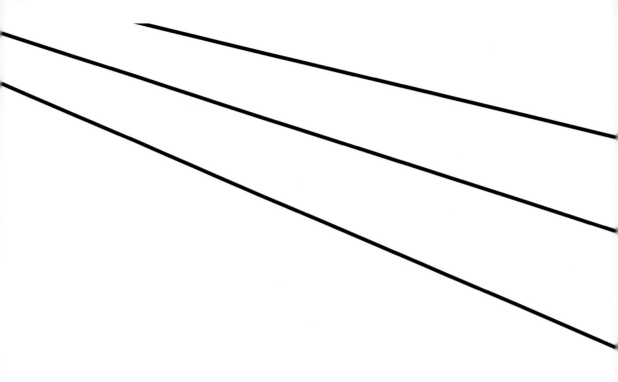

How to Help Start a
Community You Can be Part of ...

I can't tell you how to do this. Communities start and end in
so many different ways. What I can say is that my experience with
a community starts with me having been at my lowest point –
financially, artistically, psychologically – a point that largely came about as a
result of being an artist who was both alone and waiting on other people. Waiting
for someone to commission me, to programme my work, to validate my practice. And
then Andy and I had our first big year at Forest Fringe, and I realised that this wasn't a case of
Andy and I supporting artists, but a case of us facilitating a context in which we could all support
each other. Something started to gain momentum, and it began to be clear that if we worked together we
could be empowered as individuals and as a collective. The best analogy is one of those multi-pedalled
Party Bikes you see at Hen and Stag Dos. Everyone chatting and laughing until they forget that they're
peddling. It just starts to feel like the normal thing to do. Except we aren't usually drunk, and nobody is
necessarily getting married. But you keep each other going, you make each other rest, go faster, turn corners.
And when you go past people on the bike they think two things: 1. That looks fun and 2. Are they tired yet?

GET LOST

DIY IS IS A LOAD OF CRAP THAT IS EASY TO GET A HOLD OF. IT IS IS A TEMPORARY

FIX FOR A DEEP STRUCTURAL PROBLEM. IT IS CHEAP AND IT IS SIMPLY NOT GOOD ENOUGH.

Image credit: Gob Squad (*Live Long and Prosper*)

The **D.I.Y.** Aesthetic

To 'not know', to be slightly 'out of control' of what happens is revolutionary.

A 'mistake' is a moment of resistance.

It colludes us all,

Where else but the live event do you have the possibility to fail?

Failure is a collapse: of the singular into the plural.

There is no singular point of origin.

Everybody is involved.

In a world becoming ever more perfect, in which every amateur can achieve perfect simulations with the right technology, the moment of the mistake, the interference, becomes a moment of confusion.

We want the event to get all mixed up in the 'what we came here to do'. So we can't know it all.

During the making of a show called Me The Monster, we produced a small series of remakes of well-known scenes from horror films. Our intention was not to copy Hollywood cinema as perfectly as possible, but to re-film the chosen scenes ad hoc, with short cuts and stand-ins, in such a way that the movement sequences and visual compositions matched but the aesthetic, scenery and acting methods spoke a totally different language. The opening sequence of *The Shining* (a car journey through the winding streets of a snow-covered mountain landscape) was transformed in our version into a toy car being pulled with a string through a snake-like path made in a sandpit. Placing the remake and the original side-by- side proved to be astonishingly effective and pleasurable because most of the edits and movement sequences were satisfyingly in synch. It was interesting to watch the very details and 'mistakes' that became apparent in the remake that strangely revealed and demystified Hollywood and the horror genre. Especially confusing and exciting were the effects when the sound sources switched between the original and the remake and our own voices swapped with those of Jack Nicholson or Shelly Duval. Here too, as with other techniques and methods we employed, a kind of double exposure effect was obtained. Showing the remake and the original side-by-side, which is both freeing and alienating to watch and seems to suggest proximity and distance at the same time, was taken further when we started to change the order and outcomes of the original scenes. For example, when the female protagonist in Halloween runs away unsuspectingly from the evil spirit we changed it so that in our version, she turns around and approaches him, confronting him at first with a knowing look then stands in front of him, taking his mask off and touching his face. When playing both versions simultaneously, the films depart from each other at this point with our version rewriting the original and opening a new experimental area for us. While the original pauses on a freeze frame, the copy takes a turn only to reunite with the original after a short diversion. In another section, both films slow down, moving themselves at the same rate but in different directions. 'Dueting' is what we called this form of doubled screenings (sometimes synchronous, sometimes diverging).

In Hollywood films you can't tell how an effect is achieved. Letting reality in through interaction with the audience (real people, real lives) is always a risk because it means that we open up our usually contained aesthetic system to something uncontrollable. We believe that it is not only important to refute perfection, but also to give the imperfect a platform, a space. An arbitrarily composed cast of audience members or passers-by, who don't have the chance to learn their lines and who have improvised costumes and haphazard props, helps us to show how people exert themselves to achieve an extraordinary effect while failing at the same time.

We deliberately distance ourselves, through our presentation and choices of costume and props, from conventional viewing expectations influenced by Hollywood and popular television formats. When reality and fantasy images meet, this opposition and inherent discrepancy produces friction, conflict and deficiencies. We think that this is exactly where the dramatic and tragic potential of our work lies. Costumes are created from cheap flea market items that stand in for 'real' glamour and beauty. We always choose plastic pearls over real ones or a toy policeman's helmet rather than an ex-force model, because we don't intend to conceal the real person behind the glamour of photorealistic illusion. It is always a 'bad' disguise, a double exposure. There is a dialogue, a critical space between the performer and the 'character'.

In a context where beauty is normally associated with the immaculate, fragility and mistakes are transformed into another type of 'beauty', a process that we hope is liberating for those who get involved in our work.

Later (2008-9) we made Live Long and Prosper, a two-screen film that shows within it seven 'block buster' film sequences, all death scenes, restaged by seven performers across the city of Berlin. The gorilla style remakes are shown side-by-side with the original movie scenes. The devices of narrative film are doubled up and reflected back on themselves in a cinematic game of 'spot the difference'. The mountains of the Wild West become escalators in the central station, a battlefield from a historic war becomes a city fairground and the interior of the Starship Enterprise is played by Pfennigland - a cheap "Everything's a Pound" shop. The intertwined sequences and their doppelgangers weave simultaneously towards their inevitably tragic ends, leaving a trail of pretend corpses, abandoned in cinematic pull-backs that reveal everyday urban life continuing around them.

Something uncanny happens, a dialogue between the original and the remake. This dialogue is about compensating and stand-ins. There is a pleasure in observing the remake – the replacement of high-end production/location with found objects – a desert scene shot in a train station, a mountain replaced by an escalator.

It's as though one is the fantasy and the other is the compensated reality. For us, our real version is so much more satisfying – it's like when you find a real bargain in a charity shop and part of its beauty is that you found it for 50p. You need the original, or a notion of the original, in order to really get the beauty of the remake.

This construction and copy appears a lot in our work. When we copy, it is always about the friction and the confrontation of the original with the here and now. Our remakes are always just an attempt at an approximation that is purposely never quite right or one with the original, but actually presents the gaps, the mistakes and the failure of the attempt. Therefore, our remakes are never just remakes, but are almost always about the stepping into and out of those roles and situations and this becomes in itself a part of the process. The preparation work, the building up, the mechanisms of construction and deconstruction are exposed in different ways and create what interests us about this theme: the friction and discrepancy with the materials we are examining.

We want to show people attempting to do something. The attempts that we show are real. It is possible to observe us live as we follow one of our own over-ambitious or even impossible goals. You can see us work on them and despair with them, quarrel with the unpredictability of weather and traffic and the moods and temperament of audiences and passers-by. Our live films are always 'making of' films in which the situations that happen live in front of the camera are debated, commented upon and interpreted as they are openly manipulated and re-framed. The audience can see the liveness in our efforts and failures. It is a reality of coincidence and chance, the unshapeable and the unpredictable quality of reality, which meets a piece of art head on and influences it.

Were not interested in ability, but rather in the feeling of empowerment; that one empowers oneself to do something. Especially when you can't actually to it. You tell yourself, 'Even though I can't do it, or even though this is now a technically bad do-it-yourself situation, I'll do it anyway.' And this, I think, is maybe what is emotional about our work; it gives people a good feeling; it stirs them up. Because as an audience member, you have the feeling that possibilities are opening up, rather than closing. That is often the problem with ability. You see it and think, "that is perfect, but what does it have to do with me?"

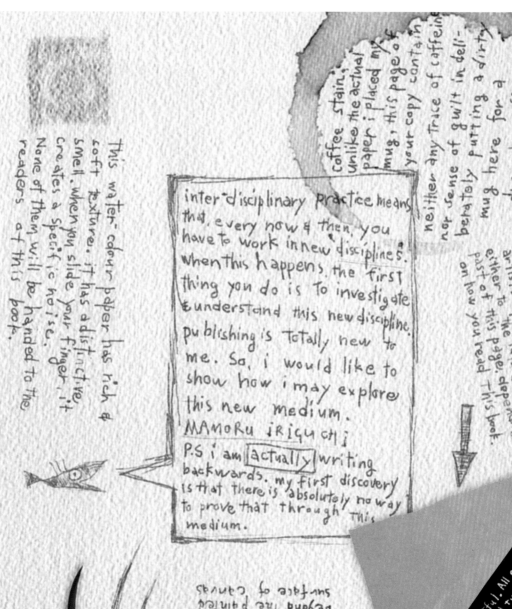

inter-disciplinary practice means that, every now & then, you have to work in new disciplines. when this happens, the first thing you do is to investigate & understand this new discipline. publishing is totally new to me. So, i would like to show how i may explore this new medium. MAMORU IRIGUCHI

P.S i am actually writing backwards. my first discovery is that there is absolutely no way to prove that through this medium.

This water-colour paper has rich & soft texture. it has a distinctive smell. when you slide your finger, it creates a specific noise. None of them will be handed to the readers of this book.

coffee stain. unlike the actual paper i placed my mug, this page of your copy contain neither any trace of caffeine nor sense of guilt in deli- berately putting a drip of mug here for a dreamatic effect.

this triangle is another artist's space that belongs either to the future or the past of this page. depending on how you read this book.

homage to Lucio Fontana who showed us that there is another world beyond the painted surface of canvas

i am forgetful. All events that happened two pages ago now belong to the world of oblivion.

Dear reader,

I get asked for advice a lot. With a modicum of success comes a belief that you are somehow in control, brimming with advice and worse still ... that you know "THE SECRET."

What secret?

THE SECRET.

The secret of how to make an excellent show. Or piece of art. Or statement.

Truth is, we are all always going to be trying to figure out that puzzle. It's the endlessness of the game of Performer Cat, Audience Mouse (or vice versa) that keeps us alive. Keeps us awake at night. Keeps us tied to a profession that has little mercy.

Truth is. There is no secret. And the sooner you get that stupid thought out of your head the better. It's a common misconception that art, particularly performance (a form that can only truly be complete with another person present but most commonly made alone) is an elusive unicorn, riding on the distant waves of sand-through-fingers land. It isn't, it doesn't skirt around the back of your eye ball constantly just out sight; it doesn't echo in a moment on the bus and then disappear before you can put your catching gloves on. It's there. Tangible. An equation. A simple theory. The best artists, you will notice, have known this for years. The best artists figure out their own theory. Getting them to share that: THAT'S a secret.

Well give me a space in a book ... that's how you get me to share SOME of mine.

The following advice can be taken with a pinch of salt. You may think I'm a cunt. Many do. But if you do take it, take it into a true heart. What do you have to lose; it might just save your life.

1. YOU ARE A HUMAN BEING

First thing's first. We are humans. We have feelings, we have souls. Don't beat yourself up about your practice. Ever. It is the self-loathing and doubt that delays EVERYTHING. Imagine yourself as a baby, if you keep being mean to a baby, it will hate you and poop out all sorts of nonsense to punish you. Take care of yourself. Be kind. Give yourself time, chocolate, holidays and a fucking break. Negativity breeds contempt. Happy artists make good art.

2. I'M GONNA READ THAT BITZH

Constantly. And I mean every second or every day of your artistic practice, feed yourself knowledge. Read journals, read books. If in doubt, or lacking in direction mother fucker ... READ. Read until something comes. It's the best bit of advice I ever got. You are essentially a monkey, the only thing that makes us better than the animals is our intellect. Swallow dictionaries, absorb data, remember all those subjects at school that fascinated you just that little bit less than drama or art and ignite your brain with them once more.

3. HAVE A STORY TO TELL

This is my hardest piece of advice BUT If you are not an interesting, charismatic, funny, charming or strange person you should NOT be making performance. Particularly solo performance. Additionally. If you don't have a story to tell something that truly ignites fires, something that blows your mind. Don't fucking tell it. So often I watch work that shouldn't have been made. No-one apart from your mum and dad thinks you are cute, cool or worth listening to. Only a mind blowing story or concept will make strangers fall in love with what you do. Up your game.

4. LIKE A FINE WINE

Know that your voice as an artist will very simply get better with age and life experience. Accept it. Your first piece of work won't be in the main house at the Barbican, you are not ready for that. Aim high long term but remember art takes time to mature. I didn't start making very public work until I was 30 because I genuinely knew my voice wasn't ready yet. I stuck to the shadows, to the club scene, to the crappy open mics, so no-one knew I was shit ... I just arrived GOOD. Don't rush it. Just go with the flow.

5. IDEAS COME NATURALLY

If something hurts your brain ... not in that pushing, surging, slowly unpicking way when you are figuring something amazing out in a show ... but like actually hurts and pains and keeps you awake. Chuck it in the bin. Nothing is worth forcing, chances are you are trying to hard to be clever. Equally know when to "fuck your darlings". If you identify that no matter how hard you try and squeeze an ideas fat ass into a show, it won't fit ... fuck it. Stick it on the shelf. It will come in handy another time. Material I made years ago is still there on the shelf waiting for its moment. Art is for life.

6. ERM ... THE AUDIENCE

This one is for the natural naval gazers. The ONLY reason you are here, on this stage ... the only reason sunshine ... is to entertain THAT audience. THE ONLY REASON. Let's not get lost window shopping in Ego Town. Don't forget that we are entertainers, all of us, forget this and the audience will tear you to pieces like a pack of hungry Alsatians. Everything you make, every turn, look, speech and action is for them. Start making everything with two things in mind ... What do you want THEM to know and how do you want THEM to feel about it. SIMPLE. If you can decide, execute and manipulate those decisions accurately then you, young Jedi, will have a long career ahead of you Masters of manipulation.

7. BRING IN THE NEW

Don't follow the herd. Lots of people will say its ok to not be totally different to everyone else. I DISAGREE. There is not enough room on the circuit or in the galleries for 5 versions of the same artists. There is only one Bryony Kimmings, the imitators (and believe me there are many) are not AS GOOD. They can't be, because whilst they are busy trying to be like me, I am trying to again and again NOT be like me. Newness. The shiny seductress of the unknown ... she is my girlfriend. Be an individual, do something completely different, why wouldn't you?!

8. BRANDING AND VISUAL IDENTITY

Just because we are artists it doesn't mean we have to be poor, un-aspirational beings clothed in hemp, drinking from jars and covered in paint. I am not having THAT, I am always impeccably dressed, I drive a Mercedes and I always have money in my account (read: CUNT). But truthfully it is actually a good racket this art shit. The way to make sure that you are the name on people's lips, that you are the one that people want to commission (as well as making killer art, which a lot of artist do very well) is to appear like the label of choice. It works just like designer branding. Make your website the slickest, make your logo the best, your images the most moreish (I spend a fortune on pictures as they sell so much better than anything I could ever write). BRAND yourself. You are a business person just as much as you are an artist. FACT.

9. LIVE YOUR LIFE

Here are some final things that should never be sacrificed for art :

Boyfriends

Fucking

Good music

Your love of shit films and stupid comics

Cooking for people

Family and dogs

Enjoying nature

Your human rights

Christmas

Friendships

10. I LOVE YOU

If you ever need me, I am here. I am serious. I know I said in the beginning that I hate being asked for advice, I sometimes say shit for effect. Call me, email me. I am here. We all are, for each other. Those are the unwritten rules, don't fuck with them.

Word to your mother.

Bry xx

Image credits: Main image and below left: Nigel & Louise, *Being Elvis*, 2013.
Below middle: Joshua Sofaer, *Soho Sideshow*, 2013.
Below right: Zierle & Carter, *At The Edge of the Land*, 2012.

DIY

- an annual scheme for artists working in Live Art to conceive and run unusual professional development projects for other artists.

Have you heard the one about the artists who went to the World Elvis Festival in Porthcawl? Or the one about the artists who spent £500 on lapdances? Or the one about the artists who went to a farmhouse and didn't sleep for a week? Or the one about the artists who trained to be professional wrestlers? Or the one about the artists who set out to see how far they could send a sound? Or the one about the artists down Mecca bingo? Or the one about the artists who created the perfect citizen robot? Or the one about the artists who staged Calamity Jane in 16 hours? Or the one about the artists and radical hairdressing, who took it personally, who hated America, who couldn't live on vitriol alone, who were imperfect, who were waterproof, who got out more often, had no regrets, and went To Gypsyland?

Chances are if you have, then you've probably participated in DIY already.

As with most things, DIY started life with the seed of an idea: in this case, an interest in the apparent oxymoron of "training" for artists (health and safety anyone?). Now in its 10th year, DIY has been providing small grants for artists to run unusual professional development opportunities for themselves and their peers since 2002. Conventional ideas of training, research and career development are often unable to effectively address how artists are supported in their artistic and professional development where process is not only critical but also inherent. Whilst the Live Art

Development Agency can provide resources, contacts and downloads galore, the professional development needs of Live Artists are so specific that it's naïve to think any organisation could do a thorough job of catering for them all. DIY provides a framework in which the tables are turned, giving the artists the power to set the agenda and enabling them to literally Do It Themselves, providing relevant professional development experiences for themselves and their peers. More often than not the most useful thing an artist can do is get their teeth into a subject, get their hands dirty exploring something, and all the better with a group of likeminded peers, which is exactly what DIY enables.

DIY is coordinated by the Live Art Development Agency, with the support and input of many national partner organisations, and is run as an open submissions scheme inviting artists to pitch outlandish, risky, unfundable (to some) and bonkers ideas all in the name of professional development. A panel of the national partner organisations whittles down the applications and then the selected artists receive £1,000 each (to cover the costs of their project) and throw open their doors to allow expressions of interest from other artists who'd like to take part. DIYs are not masterclasses: whilst the lead artist is the facilitator and organiser of their DIY they're certainly not a guru or a teacher. DIYs aren't workshops in any conventional sense. Experience shows that lead artists of DIY projects get as much out of running a DIY as the participants do, and that's why many so many artists have returned to run further DIYs in subsequent years.

This year, Rosana Cade will host her DIY *My Big Sister's Gonna Teach Us To Lap Dance* in Birmingham for a group of ten artists all interested in feminism, performance and the contemporary debates and polarized opinions around lapdancing. Over the course of the project, the artists will all receive a professional lap dance in a lap dancing venue; participate in a lap dancing workshop led by a professional lap dancer; and perform their lap dance, one on one, to another member of the group. The DIY will be further bolstered by discussion and contributions from feminist thinkers and those with experience in the lapdancing industry. This DIY was born out of a new project Cade is embarking on in which she'll make a full length show about lapdancing. In many ways it's the perfect DIY project: risky, provocative and who else is going to fund a project where half the budget is being spent on lapdances in a Brummy stripclub? The experiences from Rosana's DIY will feed directly into the making of this new piece whilst contributing to her practice more generally. I also suspect it could also be a hugely rewarding and challenging experience for all the participants – they're not just pawns in Rosana's research process.

Although the initial DIY offerings were London focused, it was important to us that it became a national scheme as there seemed to be a real demand (and by process of deduction, a real lack of) professional development opportunities for Live Artists across the country. From DIY 2 (2004) onwards we've always ensured that we've had projects running in a variety of locations around the UK. In 2013, we have 23 projects happening right across the breadth of England, Scotland and Wales, everywhere from Cornwall to Porthcawl, Liverpool to a freshwater pool just outside of Bristol. This spread of projects has meant that regardless of where an artist is based in the country, they're probably not more than an hour or so train ride away from a DIY project, though even if they are a big part of the DIY experience is getting the chance to explore a new place, with new people. There are further plans afoot to launch a number of DIYs in Ireland in 2014 in response to the boom in exciting live work being produced there, and the apparent lack of this type of opportunity.

Fundamental to the Agency's outlook is collaboration. With DIY we work with a number of partner organizations from across the country to make the scheme possible. All these partner organizations pool expertise and resources (lots of small financial contributions make up one big pot of money!) and then act as a host for one of the projects, which would typically happen in the host organisation's region. The role of the host organisation is purely to help and advise when needed, rather than lead or control the project. DIY has time and time again demonstrated that artists are extremely well equipped to conceive and manage complex and often demanding professional development initiatives. The benefit of working with host organizations is their local knowledge, be it relevant contacts for sourcing free space, good places for lunch and ways of acquiring any other vital materials the project might require, locally. Furthermore, the combined promotional muscle of having over 20 organisations shouting about the scheme gives the DIY projects a weight that they wouldn't have had, had they been happening in isolation or independently of the scheme. In line with this is the annual DIY Report for which all the participating artists feed back on or respond to their projects through words and images. The Report is widely circulated amongst funders and other 'cultural stakeholders' to raise awareness of the brilliant projects happening across the country, of the many different forms that 'professional development 'can take, and of the often extraordinary outcomes DIY makes possible.

We're always delighted when we hear (sometimes years down the line) of an outcome relating to an earlier DIY project. After Joshua Sofaer's DIY 7: *Indecent Proposal*, which took place at Yorkshire Sculpture Park, three of the participating artists have received commissions from YSP. John Jordan's influential *Response-ability* DIY in 2003 led to the birth of the *Clandestine Insurgent Rebel Clown Army*, and countless others have met artists through DIYs with whom they still collaborate to this day. In 2012, genuinely transformative experiences were reported from two workshops: Zierle & Carter's *At the edge of the land, of practice and of knowing* and Michael Mayhew's *The Body As Art*. Legendary DIYs also include Curious' *Autobiology* in 2008, which influenced a generation of new makers, and Geraldine Pilgrim's *Please keep your luggage with you at all times,* which saw participants undertake solitary train journeys with a suitcase gifted to them by Pilgrim herself. In 2012, we even had a romance between two of the participants of Dickie Beau's *Water Shouldn't Be Water* weekender, which as of Monday 9th September 2013, is still going strong.

Also intrinsic to DIY is that the chosen projects appeal to artists across a broad range of practices and at all stages of their career. Everything from physical combat to socially engaged practices, tribute acts and 'selfies' are up for interrogation by our cohort of lead artists this year, who include such influential and distinct figures as Tim Etchells, Neil Bartlett, Kira O'Reilly and Marcia Farquhar. In addition, Joshua Sofaer returns to build on the success of *Indecent Proposal* to run a project specifically for mid-career artists around pitching ideas to Soho businesses and organisations in *Soho Sideshow*, whilst Ursula Martinez will run *Don't Wait Tables*, an intensive weekend exploring ideas for short club performance, the first time she's ever led something of this nature. Artists at an earlier stage of their career leading DIY projects this year include Peter McMaster, Jesse Darling and GETINTHEBACKOFTHEVAN, and it feels particularly exciting to support this younger generation at such potentially crucial junctures in their careers. But what's most interesting is that all these DIY projects have been hugely over subscribed by artists from hugely different backgrounds and disciplines showing a real thirst for this initiative. We've had applications for participation from respected visual artists, underground performers, theatremakers, writers and more, spanning the full spectrum of art spaces from stage to gallery and beyond. All this adds up to make DIY singular and distinctive, and with it's never-say-never attitude it's become a real melting pot of people and ideas which has repeatedly produced remarkable outcomes with legacies still being felt to this day. As Manick Govinda from Artsadmin sums it up: "DIY really is an amazing initiative, yet so simple in its concept: invite artists to submit out-of-the-box ideas that address an aesthetic or socio-political puzzle, then get more artists involved to explore through various means possible propositions with other artists, sharing time together. It's a wonderful recipe for the unexpected and unusual and the joy of convivial knowledge. Often the seeds of new work are sown through trying something novel and different."

So did you hear the one about the performance artist, theatre maker and activist who went to the nudist camp?

If not, keep your eyes open for the next round of DIY projects, as the results, more often than not, are no laughing matter.

**Live Art
Development
Agency**

הוּא הָיָה אוֹמֵר אִם אֵין אֲנִי לִי. מִי לִי. וּכְשֶׁאֲנִי
לְעַצְמִי. מָה אֲנִי. וְאִם לֹא עַכְשָׁיו. אֵימָתַי׃

Hillel said: If I am not for myself, who will be for me? And when I am only for myself, what am I?
And if not now, when? ... If I am not for myself, who will be for me?

A *DIY* Religious Text Analysis on the Topic of *DIY*

Despite my complicated relationship with religion, and Judaism in particular, I always had a great admiration for those who wrote commentary on the Torah. I'm not sure when religions became, in many cases, oppressive, divisive and conservative spaces, but I like to imagine that, at least in the beginning, religious study was an exercise in DIY – a group of people coming together to try to figure out the major questions in life. Whether they honestly considered the Torah divinely written or not, I admired the process they took with it – they broke up each phrase, each word, each paragraph mark, and discussed, debated and expounded on this very simple text which (when presented without accompanying commentary) is actually quite small.

Like many other artists, I never really understand my own process or why I do, how I do, what I do. I like the mystery of it and the strange, if sometimes meandering trajectory. The urge to create has always felt quite religious to me in that no one knows where it comes from, how it is useful, and very rarely do people consider the potentially negative consequences.

As we are being asked to reflect on our process as DIY makers, I thought to follow the process of what I think of as the first DIYers, those Torah commentators that I spent so much of my childhood admiring. I thought to find a classic piece of text and interpret it with DIY aesthetics and practice in mind. It's a classic text, from Rabbi Hillel (b. 110B.C.), perhaps overdone, but its reflections on solo performance, and doing it myself, well, I hope they are clear.

Hillel said: If I am not for myself, who will be for me?

How can you not do it yourself when the work is about yourself? It may seem a basic tenant for those engaged in solo autobiographical art making, but if I don't make it, who will? And how could anyone *but* me be the creator of the work that I make?

Of course, for this interpretation of the text to be acceptable, it must be considered a good thing that I do, in fact, create work. This may or may not be true. I would like to think it's true, and sometimes colleagues, audiences, curators and funders seem to confirm my belief that the world is affected positively from the fact that I create work. Or at least there are no noticeable, negative effects.

And when I am only for myself, what am I?

If a work is solely about the creator, what is its use or function in public space, or to others? How can an artist ensure that there are access points in their work – particularly if creating autobiographical work – for others? And if a work doesn't speak to anyone outside the artist's experience, is it worth seeing / funding / promoting?

For me, solo performance was always about having faith that the experiences I have are shared in some ways to a more universal human experience, but I never know if this is really true. My process of creating, therefore, always has started with telling an idea to many people: if I have to explain it too much, the project will probably not move forward. This is not about being popular, or accessible to everyone, but I do think it is about being accessible to someone, as a matter of course.

And if not now, when?

When does one take a break from making or thinking about making autobiographical performance? If life experience is the source material, how is it possible to delineate life from seeing the world as just one long residency? And why do I feel a need to notate constantly, as if I forget this idea, or don't create this idea in the foreseeable future, my life will be unrealised or unfulfilled in some way?

When one does it themself, they are always doing it, aren't they? This doesn't mean that one need be a workaholic, or have an unhealthy relationship with art / life balance, but the constant feel of *on*-ness has been something that I've considered for the past 10 years. If you don't require others to create the work, you also can't really take a break. There are positives and negatives to this, but I'd love to find someone who Does It Themself, and who doesn't feel the need to Do It Themself all the time. A subject, when observed, does not remain unchanged… How does this work when our subjects are ourselves?

One of the reasons why I also admired those religious scholars was that they were critical enough of their own humanity and subjectivity that they knew that others, upon reading their ideas, would be [sometimes harshly] critical, and would either add to, or completely contradict what they had said. I just hope that I don't sound like I did when I was 13, fresh off my Bar Mitzvah, thinking that my philosophical meanderings were the first of their kind. I know they're not. But sometimes it is nice to do some philosophising on your own.

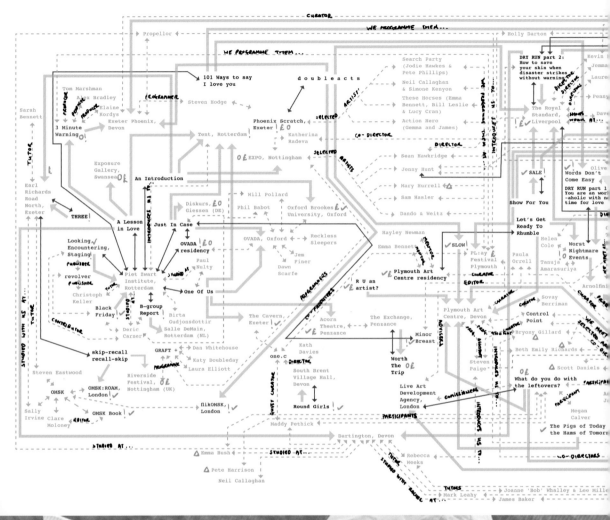

CURATOR
WE PROGRAMME THEM...
WE PROGRAMME THEM...

Propellor
Holly Darton

Tom Marshman
Alex Bradley
Elaine Kordys
Exeter Phoenix, Devon
Sarah Bennett

3 Minute Warning

101 Ways to say I love you

Steven Hodge

doubleacts

Phoenix Scratch, Exeter £0
Katherina Radeva

Search Party (Jodie Hawkes & Pete Phillips)
Neil Callaghan & Simone Kenyon
These Horses (Emma Bennett, Bill Leslie & Lucy Cran)
Action Hero (Gemma and James)

DRY RUN part 2: How to save your skin when disaster strikes without warning
Kevin
Jomma
Laure

The Royal Standard, Liverpool
Penny
Dave

Exposure Gallery, Swansea
EXPO, Nottingham
An Introduction

Earl Richards Road North, Exeter

THREE

A Lesson in Love
Just In Case

Diskurs, £0 Giessen (DE)
Phil Babot
Will Pollard
Oxford Brookes University, Oxford

SELECTED ARTISTS

Sean Hawkridge
Jenny Hunt
Mary Hurrell
Sam Hasler
Dando & Weitz

SALE
Words Don't Come Easy
DRY RUN part 1 You are an work -aholic with n time for love

Show For You

Olive

Looking, Encountering, Staging

revolver

Christoph Keller

Black Friday

OVADA £0 residency
Paul Nulty

OVADA, Oxford
Reckless Sleepers
Jem Finer
Dawn Scarfe

Piet Zwart Institute, Rotterdam

One Of Us

B-group Report

RU an artist?

Hayley Newman
Emma Bennett

SLOW

Plymouth Art Centre residency

Let's Get Ready To Rhumble
Helen Cole
Worst Nightmare Events

PL:ay Festival Plymouth
Paula Orrell
Tanuja Amarasuriya

Birta Gudjonsdottir
Deric Carner
Salle DeMain, Rotterdam (NL)
The Cavern, Exeter

Acorn Theatre, Penzance

The Exchange, Penzance

Plymouth Art Centre, Devon
Sovay Berriman
Control Point
Bryony Gillard
Beth Emily Richards

Arnolfini

skip-recall recall-skip

Steven Eastwood

GRAFT +
Dan Whitehouse
Katy Doubleday
Laura Elliott

one.c

Kath Davies

Minor Breast

Worth The £0 Trip

Steven Paige

Scott Daniels

OMSK

OMSK:ROAM, London

OMSK Book

Riverside Festival, Nottingham (UK)

flikOMSK, London

South Brent Village Hall, Devon

Round Girls

Live Art Development Agency, London

What do you do with the leftovers?

Sally Irvine Clare Moloney
EDITOR

Maddy Pethick

Dartington, Devon

Megan Calver
The Pigs of Today the Hams of Tomorro

Emma Bush
STUDIED AT...

Rebecca Weeks

Pete Harrison
Neil Callaghan

Mark Leahy
Joanne 'Bob' Whalley & Lee Mille
James Baker

CO-DIRECTORS

Tent, Rotterdam

HAVE YOU SEEN OUR WORK?
MAY 2012
*** FREE ***
LOW PROFILE ARE ~~EIGHT~~

Image credit: Oliver Rudkin (2012)

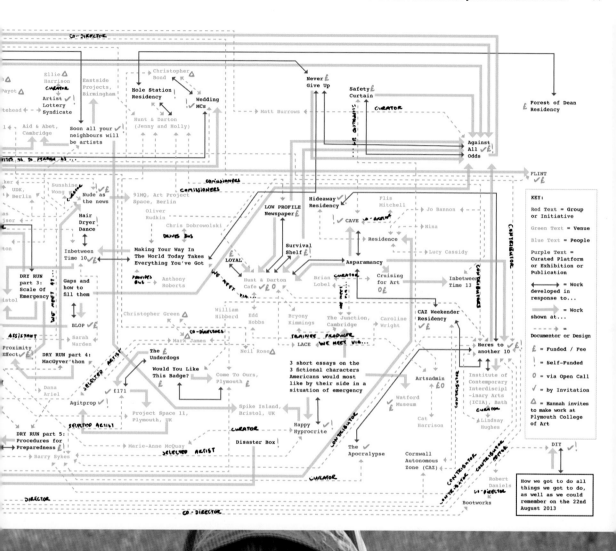

CO-DIRECTOR

Ellie △
Harrison
CURATOR

Payot △

Eastside
Projects,
Birmingham

Christopher △
Bond

**Hole Station
Residency**

**Wedding
MCs**

**Never £
Give Up**

**Safety £
Curtain**   CURATOR

**Forest of Dean
Residency**

tehead △

Artist
Lottery
Syndicate

**Soon all your
neighbours will
be artists**

Matt Burrows

**Against
All £
Odds**

Aid & Abet,
Cambridge

**Hunt & Darton
(Jenny and Holly)**

ITIES SE TO PSANDA AS

Sunshine△
Wong

CURATOR

COMMISIONERS
COMMISIONERS

**Hideaway
Residency** £

Flis
Mitchell

Jo Bannon

FLINT
£

UDK,
Berlin

**Nude as
the news** ✓ £

91MQ, Art Project
Space, Berlin

**LOW PROFILE
Newspaper** £

Nina

as
jer △

Oliver
Rudkin

CAVE CO-AGENT

CONTRIBUTOR

**Hair
Dryer
Dance**

Chris Dobrowolski

DRIVES BUS

Residence £

Lucy Cassidy

ton

**Inbetween
Time 10**

**Making Your Way In
The World Today Takes
Everything You've Got**

LOYAL

**Survival
Shelf** £

Asparamancy

**Inbetween
Time 13**

DRY RUN
part 3:
Scale Of
Emergency

**Gaps and
how to
fill them**

Anthony
Roberts

PONING BUS

**Hunt & Darton
Cafe** 0£

Brian
Lobel CURATOR

**Cruising
for Art**
0£

CONFORMATOR

bristol △

WE MEET AT

BLOP ✓£

Christopher Green △

William
Hibberd

Edd
Hobbs

Bryony
Kimmings

**The Junction,
Cambridge**

Caroline
Wright

**CAZ Weekender
Residency**

**Heres to
another 10** ✓£

ASSISTANT

Sarah
Warden

CO-DIRECTOR

Mark James △

Neil Rose △

TRAINEE PRODUCER
LACE   WE MEET VIA...

Proximity
Effect £

DRY RUN part 4:
MacGyver'thon

SELECTED ARTIST

**The £
Underdogs**

**Would You Like
This Badge?**

**Come To Ours,
Plymouth** £

**3 short essays on the
3 fictional characters
Americans would most
like by their side in a
situation of emergency**

Artsadmin
£0

**Institute of
Contemporary
Interdiscipl
-inary Arts
(ICIA), Bath**

Dana
Ariel △

£171

Agitprop ✓£

**Project Space 11,
Plymouth, UK**

**Spike Island,
Bristol, UK**

**Watford
Museum**

CURATOR

Lindsay
Hughes

DRY RUN part 5:
Procedures for
Preparedness £

Barry Sykes △

SELECTED ARTIST

Marie-Anne McQuay △

Disaster Box

CURATOR

**Happy
Hypocrite** ✓

Cat
Harrison

CONTRIBUTOR

DIY ✓£

SELECTED ARTIST

CURATOR

**The
Apocrypha**

**Cornwall
Autonomous
Zone (CAZ)**

CONTRIBUTOR
CONTRIBUTOR

CONTRIBUTOR ARTIST

**How we got to do all
things we got to do,
as well as we could
remember on the 22nd
August 2013**

DIRECTOR

Robert
Daniels △

Bootworks

CO-DIRECTOR

CO-DIRECTOR

KEY:

Red Text = Group
or Initiative

Green Text = Venue

Blue Text = People

Purple Text =
Curated Platform
or Exhibition or
Publication

⟷ = Work
developed in
response to...

→ = Work
shown at...

----- = Documentor or Design

£ = Funded / Fee

= Self-Funded

0 = via Open Call

✓ = by Invitation

△ = Hannah invites
to make work at
Plymouth College
of Art

E YOU SEEN OUR :
RK?

MAY 2012

*** FREE ***

LOW PROFILE

ABOUT: *Have You Seen Our Work?* is an art group and ever growing compendium of creative responses, recollections and partial rememberings made by audience members, peers, friends and strangers in response to the work of artists LOW PROFILE, compiled and published as a work in progress website. LOW PROFILE are currently working funding to develop an interactive, bespoke website to fit the needs (and real or the wishes

It's funny to think that we are DIY. I mean we are. I mean we are and we aren't in that we are because we make the shows ourselves and put them together ourselves and our aesthetic is what it is but I think I think I think maybe maybe we feel there is a stigma around DIY that is about tweeness and I don't think our work is twee so in that we I would say that I would say that I would say that we are not DIY in terms of the style but we are in terms of the definition of "DO IT YOURSELF."

Made In China

And we should all do it ourselves because if we don't who the fuck will and I think that all good artists do it themselves because if someone else does it for you it probably isn't very good unless they are a better artist than you and then you are just lucky that you've found someone who can do it themselves and you are just taking all the glory. Just make the things you want to make that you think is important to make and make it fucking good and it may not be to everyone's taste but if its good and dangerous and strange and brave it will be something worth something worth something worth something anything something. We are all just masses of particles floating around so we might as well make things that will change things because that thing will never change.

On that note.

We make work by talking. We both write,
in a quite traditional sense. Write words on
a page and read them out loud afterwards.
Sometimes what's on the page looks like a
script, a teen movie, a play. And sometimes
it looks like a stream of consciousness, a
list, a fragment of an intelligent but naïve
undergraduate's essay. Sometimes it looks like
a poem, an inane sketch that derives basically
all it's humour from word play like some poor
cousin of Morecambe and Wise or Spike
Milligan or Monty Python.

But the words we write are from talking
about an idea, a set of ideas, issues that
bother us, move us, make us angry or sad
or confused. The words we write stem from
long discussions about the world and how
it's fucked up, from autobiographical musings
about ourselves and how we're fucked up.
We sometimes say we make shows about big
things and small things (though does anyone
not?). We make shows about big small things
and big big things that keep us awake at night
that make us argue and hate each other.
The interplay between big things and small
things seems to be the general pattern of life,
and probably has been forever but we feel like
maybe it's magnified in our hyper-globalised
information overload world that is the world
of today. We sit in pubs and get pissed and
chat and goof with our mates, and as we do
we simultaneously watch football on one
screen, a stream of sextastic music videos
on another, and a news report on the latest
bombing on another.

We don't "devise" in the traditional sense,
in that we don't really do long improvisations
and we don't roll about on the floor. We fight
quite a lot and Jess cries and Tim gets irritated
and we write it all down, everything, all noted
in messy handwriting, barely legible notes,
things said or thought in passing, to be looked
over again and again, as prompts for more
writing, rewriting, as reminders of what the
hell the show is actually meant to be about,
until the show's finished.

We try to think up things, actions, that are
explosive messy and awfully fun awfully awful
to do on stage and we throw away all the
things we write and start over and keep the
things we like by cutting it up and shutting it
down and we push ourselves in our words in
our actions to parts of ourselves we don't like
and let us take this opportunity to apologize
to all of the people who've subjected
themselves to working with us we love you all
and we are sorry we are shitty when we make
shows but we have to be honest about our
shitty selves and here's a little secret but we're
making it up as we go along that's sort of the
point of what we do.

We know what's good and bad, what our
skills are, ok, what we want it to look like
but sometimes it seems the word process
has accidentally slipped from the world of
the factory into the world of making shows,
doesn't it?

Once we've thought up too much and written
down just as much if not more and talked
ourselves down enough dead-ends, we try
stuff. We put our collaged thoughts, actions,
fragments of text together, on the page, print it
out, and try it - with an audience. This works
better for us when we make the schedule of
when the audience comes in (not too often)
but its good to show stuff either way.

Then we start over.
Then we start over.
Then we start over.
Until we have a show.

I guess this is DIY. We are redefining our rules
our circumstance the circumstances around
us about us we are interested in violence in
representing the personal violences of the
social world around us so we make shows that
are glossy on first look and horrific on the
second third fourth horrifically rotten on the
inside about the explode or implode. Or at
lease we try to. At least we will keep trying to.

*(this was written in our typical way, whereby we
speak about the idea, then Jess writes something
then Tim adds to it, edits it and makes it generally
presentable)*

Milk Presents – Poetry, cabaret and running on the spot: devising our way

SO, WHY DIY?

There is no reason not to.
You've not got to wait for her to okay it
Or him to give you the go ahead
Or her to find the money
Or for them to give you their thoughts.
You don't need him to read over it
Or her to source it.

He doesn't hold the key to the idea, You do.

There's never only one way to make it
The only set you need is already waiting for you.
The people have been ready for years.
You've had the costumes all along.

Do it yourself because you are the right person,
right now, to say what you have to say, and make
exactly what you want to make

Image credit: Matt Bartrum

TO US DIY PERFORMANCE IS:

TIMELESS
POLITICAL
THROW AWAY
ENABLING
COLLABORATIVE

Here we will briefly talk about these five elements and end with an example of how we approach making performance in our own DIY way.

TIMELESS

DIY performance is guaranteed to survive the following:
technological advancements
funding cuts
global warming
building closures
political upheaval
fire, floods and acts of "God(s)"
war
recession
pretty much anything life throws at you

To ensure this survival you will need:
strong will
resourcefulness
belief
help
pritt stick, gaffa tape and blue tac

Under the right conditions DIY performance is timeless and can travel through decades and centuries without being 'unoriginal' or 'out-dated'. The beauty of a DIY approach to performance making is its reactionary nature, its ability to move with the time or against the time, and its ultimate opposition to trend, popularity and prevailing view points. It is for this reason that Milk Presents and DIY fit so neatly together. DIY is queer, it's constantly shifting to position itself as an opposite to what we consider the norm. Usually out of need, be that financial or political restrictions, and sometimes out of a perverse desire to mess with the world we live in — an equally valid

reason! Because of the 'do it yourself' ethos it will climb its way out of the ashes, scour bins for cereal boxes, set up stage on George Osborne's front lawn and wear nothing just to be noticed. DIY performance will do whatever it takes to travel through time so that it can continuously question the times we live in.

POLITICAL

DIY performance is fundamentally political because of its nature of being free from the need of normal constraints and structures of theatre. An artist is able to react and comment on social and political imbalances as quick as is necessary, as this form doesn't require other people/organisations to vet, manage and filter it. We have crafted our style from influences of older politically charged DIY forms, cabaret. Throughout the last century and a half, cabaret styles of performance have always had a finger on the pulse of political commentary. Cabaret has been able to quickly and bitingly react to injustices and imbalances in society throughout contemporary culture, with an obvious example being the Weimar movement.

Obviously other forms of theatre are able to comment on social issues but the informality and innovation of DIY performance makes it stick out like a throbbing thumb. It is brash, bolshie and balls-out riotous so that it can step back from the next piece of indie new writing or commercially commissioned play and stick two fingers up at the powers that be.

THROW-AWAY

For us, making DIY theatre is fast, dirty and generates a lot of material. We make a lot in a short amount of time and throw away the majority of it. Equally we may have spent many hours developing an idea, invested in the design for it and then decide to get rid of it the day before we open. Some things we make and throw away may creep back in later on in the process, or indeed in an entirely new show. A DIY approach doesn't allow for sentimental attachment or egotistical ownership and as a result the artistic product does not rely on the artist to speak for it; it will speak for itself.

ENABLING

DIY theatre is a very enabling form as the power to make rests purely with the people in the room. This means often you make from what you can find and find what you can to make what you want to. Doing it yourself quite simply frees you from the constraints you may have been taught to need – funding, auditions, commissions, reassurance, resources etc –and allows you to make what you want, when you want, how you want. It is the key to getting started when you feel like you have nothing to get started with. This is not to say that work cannot be enhanced by all these things and you may well find it easier with a lot of them. We are forever battling to maintain our DIY aesthetic at the same time as creating a performance with high production values, seamless performance and satisfying stage craft. A DIY approach should never be an excuse for a half assed show.

COLLABORATIVE

The very nature of doing it yourself might suggest that you need no one, you are a one man band, a one woman show, a solo designer-performer-director-production manager-producer-writer- technician. In fact Milk Presents have found the opposite. In our efforts to power all our lights by bicycle, to project our set on OHPs and elevate our props by Heath Robinson-like pulley systems we have had to collaborate with numerous people in order to create the illusion that "We do it all by ourselves on stage!" And this has resulted in widening our creative practice to those who are not always involved in the arts. We've collaborated with local council rubbish collectors, bike enthusiasts and catering staff as well as artists, designers and musicians. Unfortunately whether you like it or not DIY performance will make you collaborate, and no matter how much you want to be able to do everything by yourself you will find your practice is enriched by inviting others in.

MILK PRESENTS – DIY STEPS TO MAKING A SHOW

Step 1: Generate
Step 2: Sift and Cull
Step 3: Expand the ones that made it
Step 4: Start to stick together – and remember to take note of your joins, how can you piece the show together without noticing the selotape in between?
Step 5: Show something, you can't make forever.
Step 6: Generate, sift and cull again until you get exactly what you want.

MILK PRESENTS – STARTING POINTS AND ACTIVITIES TO GENERATE WORK

Speed writing is the quickest way we create a large amount our written text. We pick a topic – political issue, theoretical ideology, colour of the rainbow (whatever suits the situation) – and structure the format and time frame then see whatever comes out.
Try:

an opening phrase/sentence, such as 'I remember' – this is a trigger that you repeatedly write on the page until a thought or feeling or stream of associated words are ignited and you start to write.

whittling the subject matter down first. The more finite the idea, the more you'll have to write. A wide ranging idea/subject will inevitably create a block because there is so much to write.

limiting the time frame you have to write to a minute or two. This should just stop you writing all day. You are your own rule maker, try to see what works for you.

writing alongside others and don't be afraid to rip it all apart so you can stitch it together with someone else's.

DIY Steps to making a show

Endurance tasks have always been near the top of our list for devising. Tasks like these create ambiguous imagery that can easily be manipulated and melded together with other images to create "post-dramatic" styles of performance.

Try:

running on the spot until you can longer run and then deliver a self-penned poem of on super-heroes, supermarket shopping or Ikea furniture.

muscle tension – whilst sat, stood or lying, slowly building tension in the muscles from a resting state and overlaying a juxtaposing or complimentary piece of music. You can easily create quite disturbing, yet helpfully vague, imagery.

bedroom dancing – start dancing as though you're alone in your bedroom unseen by anyone else. Allocate a "level" to this energy and the size/space that you occupy i.e. your most energetic = 10 and the most space you fill = 10. Imagine this on a scale from 1 to 10. Try dancing to Madonna with the energy level 10 but taking up the least amount of space at level 1 – you'll look like you're enjoying the convulsions that Madge's music brings on.

Just examine the nature of human interaction and emotion then devise tasks to fake that feeling and evoke your intened emotional response in your audience.

Ten minute cabarets are how we began our devising process together. We'd give each other a topic and a ten minute time limit. The aim was to create the best political striptease, socially aware show-tune or satirical magic show you could.

Try:

flicking though the *Metro* or the *Evening Standard*, find an article – whether it's the most sensationalised or most glazed-over – and create a burlesque striptease to embody it. Scroll through *Twitter* and find a comment from the obnoxious bigot-of-the-day or the empowering celeb-of-the-month. Do a little research of your own to find out what they're talking about (140 characters doesn't give you a lot to go on). Then devise a song and dance number in response.

We hope these tasks are a easy starting to point for your process as well as an insight into a Milk Presents rehearsal room.

The first time I cried at a gig was 2 years ago. It was a gig with a mix of US and Irish emo, post-punk and punk acts one late summer evening at the Old Angel in Nottingham. Post-punk musician Koji (kojisaysaloha.bandcamp.com/[2]) was onstage and in between songs he stood and talked to the sticky, buzzing room about community; about what it meant, but also about holding it to account, about knowing when to call people out, and making a community stronger. I cried for two reasons. Firstly because to have someone stand up with a mic and give me permission to be the kind of person I am - and am often tired of being - who stands up and says 'you're one of me, but that thing you said/did was not ok', meant the world. And secondly because the amazing feeling of all those people in that tiny room living and loving and breathing the words and music about striving through the difficult process of trying to be better people filled me up. Filled me up in a way that until that point I had mainly associated with theatre.

diy punk performance

I make theatre. And games. And put on theatre in pubs, and wrote a PhD on the politics of personal to be found in interactive theatre. I make odd, pervasive performance pieces; stuff you download and walk through a specific city listening to, an audio piece for the top deck of a bus at 1am in London, pick-up-and-play games, installations for swimming pools, or a simple storytelling piece made for a pub back room where I stand in my protest gear and talk about having a policeman for a father.

When people ask me what kind of theatre I make I haven't really got an easy answer, but I've realised recently that if I identify with anything, it's what I would call 'DIY theatre'. In that little sweaty room in Nottingham at the beginning of Autumn, I felt the radical resonances between two worlds I love; music and performance - albeit one where I am a maker, and the other an audience member — and since then I have thought that 'theatre' isn't actually the important bit, it's the 'DIY' that interests me. I often wonder, for example, why a small pub theatre is more likely to see itself on a spectrum that ends in the National, than it is a plane that includes the gig space next door.

Daniel Yates of Exeunt Magazine sums up 'DIY' as "small scale, culturally distinctive, alternative producers of experience"[3] - following that definition the ethics of DIY is something born of a place and community,

Image credit: Victoria Melody performing *Major Tom*, photo by David Wilson Clarke

and which offers a distinct alternative to the monoculture that thrives on top-down structures, (the mainstream music industry e.g.) and 'one size fits all' models of entertainment.

I co-ran an event at the Edinburgh Festival in 2011 called '*Edgelands*'[4], in it theatre maker Tim Crouch talked about monoculture, the problems of monoculture, and the best weapon we have against it; the alternative. Any alternative. All of the alternatives[5]. DIY, in my opinion, is the best alternative there is, because it's by definition grown and shaped as a certain place to fit and make room for the people that want to live in it. Critiques of the scalability of such models are redundant in this context; one top down system and thousands of homegrown rule-set[6] variants meet in the middle.

The quote at the head of this article comes from a booklet given out by theatre-maker Chris Goode[7] at an early version of his show *Keep Breathing*. The scratch (work in progress performance) happened in a dusty old factory re-named Stoke Newington International Airport[8] (now sadly defunct, they were forced to make way for developers). A place where I and many others have rehearsed and performed for free, worked on the bar, donated furniture, paid for tickets, bought drinks, borrowed books, cleaned up, and tried to remember what goes in a Dark and Stormy[9] as someone presses a sticky £5 note into your hand.

Action Hero[10] are a theatre company that got bored of struggling to fit their work into mainstream theatres, so made 2 pieces for bars, and another for music venues. Their home is the 'Milk Bar' in Bristol - shared with other members of the collective Residence[11] - which is a disused building borrowed from the council where several companies work and support each other's work. Also sometimes they hold parties.

theatre belongs to everybody... ideas belong to no one - chris goode[1]

The Forest Fringe[12] has become the highlight of most of contemporary theatre's Edinburgh festival, and until 2012 filled the community-owned not-for-profit Forest Cafe building with performers and volunteers, who all work for food and accommodation only. Forest Fringe do parties too. Parties are important.

While the closing of the Forest and of STK mark the pressure of monoculture to close down such spaces[13], the practices of the artists of STK, and Forest Fringe continue, and so too do Action Hero. Action Hero are expressly DIY. James Stenhouse, one half of Action Hero alongside Gemma Paintin writes that:

Image credit: Fergus Evans performing My Heart is Hitchhiking Down Peachtree Street, photo by David Wilson Clarke

I would identify the work that Gemma and I do as Action Hero very much as DIY but there's an important distinction to made between two ways of using that terminology. There is much talk in theatre of a 'DIY aesthetic' and its a phrase often used to describe our work (I think we even use it to describe ourselves on our website) but the DIY element of our work is not 'an aesthetic' it comes from a genuine do it yourself approach. We sometimes do make decisions to deliberately use things that are lo-fi because of the way it changes the relationship an audience has with the work but more often than not its a genuine response to trying to make something with very few resources. So not an aesthetic choice as such. What interests me more is the punk use of the term DIY which doesn't mean 'ooh look their set is made from cardboard' but is about an approach and a way of working that deliberately avoids mainstream modes of production.[14]

It is exactly this resistance to 'mainstream modes of production' that I suggest is at the heart of a useful and radical definition of DIY. And a shared definition between many forms of DIY - music and theatre being the ones that here interest me.

In beginning the *Performance in the Pub*[15] [PitP] experiment in Leicester I set out to bring those two communities together; to learn from the music community and bring theatre to a gig going community in a gig venue, presenting experimental DIY performance work that otherwise they were unlikely to encounter. Not because they didn't want to, or couldn't understand it, but because it just happened in places they largely didn't go. There were 9 PitP events, over a year and a bit. The tagline was pay-what-you-can nights out for people who don't really do theatre. And like much of DIY work, in eschewing mainstream modes of production, it found a way of operating that relied on an ecology[16] of generosity.

The Crumblin' Cookie[17] (the venue) stopped charging me a deposit after the first event, fed me and artists from their kitchen, and occasionally wrote off the odd bar tab. Both me and the artists worked for free. Working for free is massive problem in limiting access to artistic careers, so this did trouble me, but if I did pay ITC minimum, I'd have to have gone for Arts Council funding, and then, frankly, it would be a vastly different project[18]. Not least because of what the generosity that all those artists offering something for an audience in that context represents, but also because of the deal as producer I strike up as a supportive testing ground for work-in-progress — I have to make sure I'm offering something else, if I can't offer money.

I used the format (used elsewhere in, for example, the early efforts of Hatch[19] in Nottingham) of pairing one work in progress with one more finished piece. This meant that the showings opened up process as well as presented 'product' - artists were able to test their shows, and audience members were able to get a 'band demo' style experience of a piece of work. I used language in copy that was conversational, asked artists to describe their work like they would in the pub to a mate, and got gig poster designers to do the posters. I used music terminology, and found many parallels:

What Kind of Performance? [...] Just stories really. I mean, that's what most theatre and performance is. I'm saying 'performance' here, because most of it won't be like a 'proper play'. It'll be stuff people made with their whole bodies in a room - trying ideas and stuff out until they found something that worked. Think of how bands put music together compared to how composers do [...][20]

And the audience, too were asked to be generous. By operating on the online music-world phenomenon of 'pay what you can' (emerging in response to the ubiquity of filesharing and streaming[21]) *PitP* tried to remove as much of the risk surrounding live work as possible. Not the risk in the work - but the risk around it - all you had to give in the end, was your time. But I (hopefully) spoke to you in language that you felt you belonged in, you were going to a venue (pub/gig room) that most people feel at home in, you weren't spending money if you didn't want to, and the way I introduced each show, and my curatorial process, hopefully also exposed the inner workings of how and why it was all put together. I also posted a detailed breakdown of each show cost on the walls of the venue, and how I calculated the 'break even' figure - which, if you weren't sure what to pay, gave you a figure to cleave to (by the by, every show's mean average donation was above that point).

There's a criticism of both these theatre and music DIY spaces; that they can be unscalable, insignificant[22], hard to find, and cliquey. The way you solve this is you invite everyone to build their own alternative, and you legitimise alternatives in the first place. You open up process as well as product. You pull the arts off its pedestal.

What does that mean, in practice? When you make a
space, think about how people find you. Check that
when you protect your space, you're not guarding it.
Think about how you share skills and spaces for new
things and people. Think about who's not in the room, and
why they might not feel able to be.[23]

Theatre can learn from DIY music. Theatre still operates, for
the most part, on a distribution system that is hundreds of years
old. Big, old, dedicated buildings, weighed down by running and
staffing costs. It's time to leave these, or use them differently (the
homeless and brilliant National Theatre of Wales[24] is a case in point).
All arts and creative practice would benefit from an end to the venue
divisions. By forming new kinds of venue, where performance, music,
installations, craft, libraries, kids' groups, dance classes, poetry,
printmaking, film screenings, raves, gigs, rehearsals, food and drink all
happen under one roof[25].

Theatre can also learn from the relationship bands have with their audiences. I
never heard of anyone getting a theatre company logo tattoo, or proudly, identity
define-ingly sticking up show posters in their bedroom. If merch and sales of
music that people can otherwise get for free are the main way you make any
money[26], then you have to really drive at your relationship with your fans, you
do it for them. You don't make it for them, but you play it for them, and if
you've got any sense, you're grateful if they listen. Theatre often fails at
most social media, online and audience communication because the price of
failure is not the end of their existence. Music is at its smartest when it
knows it's nothing without its community.

I call *PitP* DIY not because it eschews subsidy[27], but because it's a part
of that communality which is opposed to mainstream top-down forms of
culture and consumption. Which brings us back to "Theatre Belongs to
Everybody; Ideas Belong to No One"[28] - it's a room where everyone is
sharing a risk, everyone trusts one another a little bit, everyone is
being generous. That space belongs to everybody, and the ideas in it
are shared and taken away and changed and picked apart and left on
the tablet with a soggy beermat and carried away like a newly
discovered talisman. I describe DIY as a being together, a
practice of holding a space together, of active listening and holding one another to
account - so you believe you might have the power to have an effect in the room in the
first place.

DIY is not anti subsidy - nor am I, subsidy has advantages and drawbacks. All art
should pay a living, where it can. But living ≠ money. When you break up that
connection you're breaking away from another mainstream mode of production. Even if
just for a little while. If in PitP as an artist I get a chance to develop my work, a
space to do it, and people to talk to about it with, maybe that's worth my time.
Especially when the donations from the audience, and a bit of the organiser's money
feed me, and cover all transport and accommodation. Then, really, all anyone in that
equation is trading in is time. Time and the willingness to give it. I made a loss in
the end. If you talk about in monetary terms[29]. But the net gain in all the other ways
we value; laughter, thought, images, experiences and ideas, was far greater.

So for me, DIY is a form of collective, radical loss[30]. Or in other terms; generosity.

Image credit: Greg Wohead performing *The Many Apologies of Pecos Bill*, photo by David Wilson Clarke

1. Goode said this in a zine that he he handed out at the end of an early Keep Breathing scratch at Stoke Newington International Airport.
2. Listening to him recorded I wasn't too fussed, but live he was something else.
3. bit.ly/diyyates accessed 27th July 2013
4. flashconference.co.uk - the Edgelands content will be up for as long as we don't do another pop up conference.
5. bit.ly/crouchmonoculture
6. I use this in the game-play sense. A system is a rule set in motion, a monoculture is a system that plays out according to a single rule set.
7. chrisgoodeandcompany.co.uk
8. www.stkinternational.co.uk/
9. The answer is 'mostly rum'.
10. www.actionhero.org.uk
11. residence.org.uk/
12. www.forestfringe.co.uk/
13. Why this happens is often due to their success - in regenerating an area, or in becoming visibly present and Noticed. This is a substantial discussion for another article.
14. James Stenhouse. Dec 2011. Originally by email, but permission given to publish on hannahnicklin.com - bit.ly/jamesemaildiy
15. performanceinthepub.co.uk
16. I'm deliberately using this word in place of what might have been 'economy'.
17. www.thecrumblincookie.co.uk
18. Also it would be a big 'fuck you' to all of the underground DIY music scene folk putting on gigs that would never be able to approach the Arts Council to do similar. If I had time to raise local sponsorship, I definitely would have. But solidarity with an art form that is half of my life, and that I properly love, was important.
19. hatchnottingham.co.uk
20. I wrote this in answer to 'what kind of performance' in 'About' on performanceinthepub.co.uk/about
21. Born out of the notion that if people are downloading and streaming your music for free anyway, why not offer them the opportunity to do so in a space where you invite them to encounter you, understand what goes into it, and to provide them with the opportunity to pay what they can, or what they want.
22. But who defined "significance' as always meaning impactful on a large scale? Give me 50 people whose lives are changed over 500 whose time is filled, any day.
23. Like it or not, the fact that those who take public money are required to show how it serves the public makes theatre ask the question (though it's rarely answered perfectly).
24. nationaltheatrewales.org
25. Places like the ones that have been taken from us, the Forest in Edinburgh, or STK in London. Places like ARC in Stockton, or The Albany, in Deptford, where people from the community go in for a cup of tea, as much as to see anything.
26. Touring, in the experience of the many internationally travelled bands I know rarely breaks even on tickets/fees vs. travel/accomm/expenses.
27. I'm not assuming it would have got it, either, had I applied to it.
28. Goode said this in a zine that he he handed out at the end of an early Keep Breathing scratch at Stoke Newington International Airport.
29. One, I'd wager, that wasn't that different as a % of outlay than any subsidised building or programming activity.
30. Radical loss is a phrase I've heard Andy Field use in conversation before, though he, I'm sure, has his own definition for it.

The DIY aesthetic:
SOMEWHERE BETWEEN A HOBBY AND A JOB

My Dad and I are terrible at DIY. We are amateurs. I remember him trying to put shelves up when I was a child and he would inevitably stab himself with a screwdriver or drill through a wire or a water pipe before shouting 'For crying out loud.' I inherited his lack of DIY skills and his love of amateur dramatics. Amateur comes from the Latin for love and amateurs perform because they love it. In 2006, I left a theatre company and started an MA in a bid to remember why I loved making theatre. I made a devised performance called *Acts of Communion* (2006) with an amateur dramatics group in a church hall as part of my MA. It was the amateur dramatics group I had performed with for the first time as a child. When I was young my Dad would take me backstage and I would see the reality

behind the illusion. The make up in the dressing room. The wind-up telephone in the wings. The hand-painted scenery behind a window.

When I was 12 my Dad invited me to perform in my first amateur production. I remember waiting to go onstage, the heat of the lights and the weight of the make up. The lanterns were often gaffer taped to the walls. The curtains were drawing pinned to the ceiling. Hanging beneath the hand painted fire exit sign blu tac-ed to the ceiling. I remember the hand painted fire exit sign because I painted it with my mum when I was a child. It was a DIY proscenium arch made of A4 paper, green paint and blu tac. Its unfinished edges. The green paint bleeding into the page. It was like the plays that took place beneath it. Marked by an absence of professionalism. In *Breaking the Rules*, David Savran writes about how the early work of the Wooster Group had the aesthetic of amateur high school plays and this amateur aesthetic continues to permeate the work of Forced Entertainment, Reckless Sleepers and most recently Action Hero. [i]

When I was interviewed for my place at Lancaster University I was asked to talk about the last performance I had seen. I talked about my Dad's last amateur play. My mum was the prompt. She would sit in the wings with the script in her hand. In shows I went to as a child she would often have the most to say as performers forgot their lines. Tim Etchells writes about how when he visits the theatre he is drawn to the face of the prompt, or stagehands waiting in the wings, or lanterns, more than the actors he is supposed to be watching.[ii] Like the fire exit signs, it is the things we are not supposed to see that attract us the most. These are reassuring glimpses of reality in a world where everything else is trying to be make-believe.

Once my Dad asked me to operate the lights for their show. I anticipated there being a number of lighting cues and having to follow the script. When I arrived he told me he wanted me to switch the lights on and off at the wall. I was an amateur technician. Amateurs are unpaid and often turn to drama as an escape route. It is an

Image credit: Julian Hughes

exit strategy from the everyday. AN magazine states that: '… being amateur allows one to enjoy the act of doing as much as, if not more than, the outcome' and concluded that 'the freedom of the amateur is the freedom of the beginner: to be curious, open and fearless in the face of the unforeseen'.[iii]

Working with my Dad on my first touring project, *The Post Show Party Show* (2008), a theatrical reenactment of how my parents met during an amateur dramatic production of *The Sound of Music*, he would say; 'An amateur practises until he gets it right. A professional practises until he can't get it wrong.' He has 40 years of experience performing as an amateur. I have 15 years of experience performing as a professional. I call it a job. He calls it a hobby. But we both do it for the love of it. It was not so much Do It Yourself as Do It Together as we made the show over coffee and cake and, in doing so, I rediscovered my love of performing.

Now we are working together again on another performance called *The Middle* (2013), the final part of a trilogy deconstructing Shakespearean texts. My Dad sits at an old desk and tells the audience about learning *Hamlet* when he was at school. Hamlet is a character caught in a limbo between 'to be and not to be' and by casting my Dad in the title role I hoped to explore time passing, ageing and the relationship between father and son. The performance takes place in a foyer, between the outside and the inside, the real world and the theatre. I bubble-wrap him and we re-enact a photograph of him blindfolded walking the plank on holiday in Malta in 1967. He tells the audience he is somewhere in between the sky and the sand, jumping and falling, the memory and the photograph.

The amateur is always somewhere in between a hobby and a job, living and loving, trying and failing, the onstage and the offstage, and I like to think that when we work with the vocabulary of DIY theatre we are working with this endless potential for life and love, attempt and failure. Perhaps in the current financial and artistic climate we have, as artists, a tacit responsibility to be making work that can be performed with or without funding. However, if we are true to the spirit of the amateur, we will always have the freedom of the beginner: to be curious, open and fearless in the face of the unforeseen. We will do it because we love it.

[i] Savran, D. (1986). *Breaking the rules: The Wooster Group*. New York: Theatre Communications Group Inc.

[ii] http://www.theguardian.com/stage/2009/oct/ 29/tim-etchells-performance-theatre

[iii] The art of amateurism, *a-n Magazine*, Debate feature, February 2009.

Residence is a collective of 17 artists who share space, resources, knowledge and opportunities. We are united by a curiosity towards each others practices, and a commitment to supporting each other.

We are also friends, who have known each other for ten years or so. We share the good times; parties, conversations, dinners, sharing's of work, successful funding applications, contacts, pregnancies, births, 40th Birthdays. We also share the bad times too; unsuccessful applications, rejections, getting stuck, not getting a response, running out of energy, not having a pension. This helps us to not feel alone, to persevere, to push, to continue.

Now we are thinking about ways we can talk back, stand up and be a collective force for change. How we can use our experiences to shape better working practices and conditions for all artists. We've been thinking about collective power, unions and open letters...

Here is the first attempt at a letter written in response to a real situation experienced by some of Residence artists:

Residence
11 St Nicholas Street
Bristol
BS1 1UE

Dear ▮▮▮▮▮

We are writing to you about a ▮▮▮▮▮▮▮ that we took part in, as part of
▮▮▮▮▮▮ We are
▮▮▮▮▮ which was presented as ▮▮▮▮▮▮▮▮▮
writing to you as a collective in order to outline some concerns and bring to your
attention that ▮▮▮▮ was an experience that proved difficult for us, as artists, and
in our opinion raises more general, ethical questions and concerns surrounding
working practices for artists and arts organizations.

This was an event that relied heavily on unpaid volunteers, which we believe
certainly has value within a carefully considered structure, but has to tread a fine
line between an experience that has value for the participants not only the
organization. In this case we felt that the treatment of your volunteers bordered on
exploitation and the situation they were placed in made us uncomfortable. The
project survived on the goodwill of ▮▮▮▮▮ artists, and the unpaid efforts of
volunteers.

During our time working on ▮▮▮▮ we saw and heard a lot of discussion around
supporting new and emerging artists, alongside the presentation of ▮▮▮▮▮
work. It was clear that certain funding had been given on this expectation, but in our
experience, and that of the other artists participating in ▮▮▮▮▮▮ this
did not manifest itself or ring true.

We were made to feel ungrateful for raising our concerns during ▮▮▮▮ that the
opportunity to work alongside high profile artists such ▮▮▮▮▮ and ▮
▮▮▮▮ should offset any genuine grievances or concerns. We struggled with a
hierarchical structure that venerates largely absent, celebrity artists as we believe in
working in ways that celebrate performance and art as a place for collaboration and
participation.

Yours Sincerely,

residence

DON'T
DO IT YOURSELF

... Do It With As
MANY People
As You Can

Do it with the junior schoolteacher who is still waiting to see you on EASTENDERS
Do it with the Career's Advisors who say, "HAVE YOU THOUGHT ABOUT THE SCIENCES?"
Do it with the BABYSITTER
Do it with FRIENDLY faces and KIND words over coffee/tea/beer/cake/dinner
Do it with your PARENTS who think you should be doing something else
Do it with your parents friends who still DON'T REALLY UNDERSTAND what it is that you are doing
Do it with STRANGERS you meet in the street
Do it with people who like to WATCH
Do it with ANYONE who'll listen
Do it with your next-door NEIGHBOUR
Do it with anyone else who's doing it in the SAME city
Do it with people on the OTHER SIDE of the WORLD
Do it with someone you haven't seen in a long time on SKYPE, on the PHONE, via EMAIL
Do it with your colleague sat in your DATA ENTRY temp job with your sneaky second screen open
Do it in the EVENINGS, with someone you like, after the day job, when your brain is TIRED and your eyes are SORE
Do it with people who KEEP you DOING IT
Do it with SHOULDERS to CRY on
Do it with someone who you TRUST
Do it with someone who trusts YOU
Do it with someone you LIKE
Do it with someone you LOVE
Do it with someone in the MIDDLE of the NIGHT when you should be sleeping
Do it with a LOVER at home, in the KITCHEN, in the BATH, on the SOFA, in the GARDEN
Do it ALL THE TIME
Do it AGAIN and AGAIN and AGAIN and AGAIN and AGAIN
Do it with someone who KNOWS what you're thinking without you saying a word
Do it with the RIGHT person
Do it with people who are trying to do THE SAME THING as you
Do it with people who CAN DO things you CAN'T DO
Do it with people who SAY what they MEAN
Do it with people who have seen it ALL before
Do it with first timers with FRESH EYES and OPEN MINDS
Do it with people who are BETTER at it than you
Do it with people who have SEEN and DONE things you haven't
Do it with people who NEED you
Do it with people YOU need
Do it with people who give you little bits of MONEY
Do it with people who have REHEARSAL SPACE or any space that's bigger than your front room
Do it with people who are good at talking to people who have little bits of MONEY and REHEARSAL SPACE
Do it with people outside on a FIELD with the WIND and the RAIN and the GRASS
Do it with someone at the MOTORWAY services, at the TRAVELODGE, on the MEGABUS and with all the stuff you've bought from TESCO EXTRA or WILKINSONS
Do it at University with lots of DIFFERENT people
Do it with your personal BANKER
Do it with your ARTS COUNCIL Officer
Do it with LOCAL GOVERNMENT
Do it with someone who PAYS you
Do it with someone for FREE
Do it with STRANGERS who have never seen or done anything like it before
Do it with STRANGERS who didn't know it even existed
Do it with someone you always DREAMED of doing it with
Do it with someone you NEVER dreamed you would do it with
DO IT with EACH OTHER because if you didn't, you don't know what you would do and you don't know HOW you would DO IT

The Artisan

Sophie and Eleanor walk through the streets of Walthamstow late at night carrying a plastic Wendy House. They are also dragging two suitcases: one, violently pink, the other, leopard-print. Sophie stops. She puts down two sides of the Wendy House. She sighs.

'What is this? A job? A hobby? What?'

No answer. She picks up the Wendy House and they continue to walk.

They haven't yet reached the Overground. Walthamstow to Bethnal Green: no barriers, so it's the perfect route to sneak an oversized prop onto public transport late at night because they don't own a car and cannot afford a taxi. After that, the one mile walk to the venue for their first performance of *Cathy's Kitchen*.

Cathy's Kitchen was rehearsed in kitchens, bedrooms, living rooms, scout huts, pubs, bandstands and outhouses. A performance set in a domestic environment, it was also created from the objects found in those environments, from the props the personas use on stage, to the childhood stories they rework and regurgitate in the performance text. It is a performance which explores autobiography and how you are structured by your childhood environment.

It suits intimacy.

What is this? A job? A hobby? What?

A call home:

'What did you do today dad?'

'Nothing much.'

'Just pottering?'

'Pottering. I finished putting up the units in the kitchen last week. Your mother wants me to move on to the utility room, but I can't get the washing machine to lie flush, because each time someone replaced it before they just added another tap, so I had to cut off the whole length of pipe. I've replaced it now, but I'll need to re-plaster the wall when I'm done.'

'Sounds like a whole day's work to me dad.'

'Oh nothing much, I'm just a bit slower these days.'

Children of the children of the 50s. In the Irish and Scottish working classes the parents of those families really had to fare for themselves. We now have a choice. Thanks to state-funded education our parents had options and, thanks to state welfare, relative security.

The skills are being gradually diluted. Eleanor's father can rewire and replumb a house. He built a boat in their back garden. Eleanor can just about change the washer on a tap. But there is still the trace of something which manifests itself in a refusal to take it easy. It is an inherited work ethic. An inability to be satisfied with something we find dissatisfying. The desire to hone. To take ownership.

Dull thuds are heard through a thin bedroom wall.

'Sophie! What are you doing?'

More thuds.

The door opens to show Sophie pressed against a cupboard 6 feet high and 5 feet wide. There is a screwdriver on the floor. She has already removed the cupboard's doors, and now she is using her body weight to slide the rest of the cupboard across the room. Bruises are appearing on her arms.

'I thought it was time for a change.'

'Do you need help?'

'No.'

Stubborn.

It is an inherited work ethic. It is also at times unrealistic; unsustainable. It uses your time, your energy, your money. There are easier ways. It makes us tough.

At first it was unconscious. Then it was a necessity. Now it is a choice.

Chance played a great part in SHATTER RESISTANT's formation.

The selection of eclectic rehearsal spaces used in the development of the show weren't because we thought these spaces would make the show **better**. We were both between employment at the time and those were the spaces we could afford.

Undoubtedly, however, these surroundings influenced the show. We picked up the objects around us to play with (bananas, shoes, a Wendy House) and soon these objects became our props.

The show requires no technical assistance for sound or lighting, because none was available to us.

The show had to fit into suitcases so that we could wheel it to venues and to each other's houses. Sometimes we would take our show to work with us, storing it under a desk, or behind a counter, ready for evening rehearsals.

Now things are shifting. We don't really want to carry the Wendy House everywhere. It is, frankly, painful. Just because this show has little technology on stage, it does not mean that as artists we will not explore the effects of lighting and sound in the future. We would like to collaborate with people with different sets of skills to allow us to push performances in new directions.

Our ethos, however, will be the same. We find there is something to be said for having sole ownership over what you have made. You are your own small business manager: being entrepreneurial, while expanding your craft and making money if it helps you to survive.

What is this? A job? A hobby? What?

In an email conversation with Eleanor, many months after the night walk from Walthamstow to Bethnal Green, Sophie comes back to her own question:

I guess I feel that making performance helps me to make sense of my world. I need to construct narrative to find conclusions within my own. Therefore, creating and surviving are not cause-and-effect but, more of a 3-legged race. Watching 2 people run is exciting, but watching 2 people tied together with a piece of string falling, laughing, hurting and eventually running together is way more satisfying.

And that, my friend, is Doing It Ourselves.

ALIEN

Alien + Ridley Scott's commentary from the original Region 2 DVD release, forms the basis of the Sleepdogs artistic playbook.

We've never been concerned with doing things 'properly'; we just want to make our work interesting. So everything we do is guided by what we love, what we care about, what we want to share with other people.

We love films. Aesthetically, *Alien* is a mega-influence on Sleepdogs, and probably a greater influence on our theatremaking than our filmmaking: the way it uses light (often heavily from one side, pulsing, lots of use of flare and darkness), the way its uses sound and score, frames people and objects, its collage of mixed formats; all these elements alongside words and action as part of an integrated storytelling toolkit. If everything we made was as gripping and beautiful and immediate as *Alien*, we'd be very happy.

We first listened to the *Alien* DVD commentary in 2002, about a year after we started making our first project together: a short film called *I Will Do It For Science* (which we're still in the process of finishing). A good DVD commentary is a like a voice inside your head that tells you anything is possible. And the best thing about commentaries is that, because they unfold as the film is played, it's the film itself that contextualises the insight.

When we talk about our work, we often find ourselves referencing both *Alien*, the film, and its DVD commentary (specifically the original Region 2 DVD commentary – the one on the Quadrilogy box-set is different, guys.) So when thinking about the DIY-ness of our practice, we thought we should re-watch it and acknowledge the tricks, tactics and attitudes of Mr Scott and his collaborators that we've absorbed into our process, and which have directly influenced particular projects.

SPOILER ALERT: As well as containing plot spoilers, the following probably won't make much sense if you don't know the film. If you haven't seen *Alien* yet, watch it. It's brilliant.

This isn't a rulebook. The timestamps are approximate.

00.00.00 Ridley Scott sparks up a cigar. He says "hello." Just him. Feels a little like he's in the room with us.

00.02.15 studio complained about nothing happening for the first 45 minutes. Scott's response: "Nothing happens for the first 45 minutes – that's the whole point. Because when it does start happening, you've really got to HAVE people."

Pauses and longueurs are all part of the music of the experience. Maybe nothing 'Hollywood' happens for 45 minutes but we get the characters, situation, frustration, soundtrack… **Directly influenced:** *Astronaut,* where for the first third of the show nothing happens except the burbles and static bursts of Apollo communications.

00.07.42 Scott deliberately mixed the sound in the breakfast scene to muffle and overlap the dialogue. He always feels uneasy when he can't clearly hear what people are saying, and wanted to stir a similar sense of uneasiness in the audience.

A creative decision driven by raw emotion as opposed to any sense of artistic propriety. It's not about doing it properly – it's about making the experience work; making something in the manner of how you want it to *feel.* **Directly influenced:** *The Bullet And The Bass Trombone,* much of which is about not knowing and not understanding – whole sections of the story involve badly recorded conversations being simultaneously translated, breakdowns in communication, a narrative in pieces.

00.10.10 we're told just enough about each crewmember to know who they are and where they stand in the 'class' system of the crew.

If this kind of economy can work in film, there's no reason it can't work in theatre too. We're told barely anything about the characters' lives, but we know just enough to feel scared out of our wits on their behalf. **Directly influenced:** *The Bullet And The Bass Trombone,* where there's an entire orchestra to introduce, describe and follow. We did it through very carefully chosen details – scant, sometimes one single fact apiece, but always specific and carefully framed.

00.10.50 nothing happens for 45 minutes, but Jerry Goldsmith's score sustains the tension. After that 45 minutes, "because of the score, the audience is so sprung loaded, it's easy, it's rock'n'roll"

And the music isn't always scary. Often it's eerie, sometimes it's beautiful. Sometimes it's your typical space music. The point is: it accumulates.

00.12.08 The casting process took a really long time, but "if you cast it right, there are so many other problems in filming… The better your cast, you've got 50% of your problems over on the day."

Not only has the right cast made the process smoother, it's meant the end result is better. 'Cos that's what it's about right? It's not just about getting it made; it's about making it great for an audience. **Directly influenced:** *1-2-3-4-.* Whilst *1-2-3-4-* was a short film, we cast it from the local performance and music scene. We didn't worry about people's experience working to camera, or learning scripts; we just wanted to be confident that they could hold attention and be funny. We had to wait several months for everyone to be available at the same time, but it was worth it for the fun we had on the day and the results we got on screen.

00.12.35 "They were a great crew. They all worked really well as a team. Maybe due to the sets, we all felt like we were making something special"

The physical space you work in influences the way you work. **Directly influenced:** *All My Dreams on VHS,* a short film about lust and anachronistic technology. We couldn't do much to the location, but we brought in one remarkable set piece that we'd spent days lovingly creating: a stack of 1600 hand-labelled VHS tapes. It made a very tight shooting schedule 1000% more fun and quickly gave the temporary crew (we'd borrowed them for the weekend from the team filming *Skins*) a shortcut into the tone and humour we were aiming for. The labels were titles of dreams like: *BRAINTROUSERS* and *GO TO SEE CONCERT ON UNDERSTANDING IT'S CLASSY + SOPHISTICATED BUT IT'S JUST CHICKENS IN FUCKING WAISTCOATS*. It got a bunch of international festival screenings and won us a camera, which meant we could make more films.

00.16.25 The tight schedule meant they had to shoot the cockpit fire in a day. "But with sound effects, and shooting into lights, and of course, the actors, I think we conveyed the sense of chaos."

This comes at the end of a whole section where Scott talks about things not being quite right – having to try all sorts of stuff, work with basic kit and models, "dodgy exhausts", experiment, work it out. Lots of doubt. Phrases like, "but I guess… you can buy it". There was clearly lots of uncertainty in the process, but the intent was always clear, and despite having to work it out as they went along, the end result totally sells it.

00.17.20 "I still love the process of operating [camera, literally being the person behind the camera] because you can invent while you're doing it."

He may be talking about camera operating, but isn't this the process of putting yourself in the audience, whatever it takes? We've found that taking the effort to re-block our shows for different spaces, sometimes taking up almost as much rehearsal as it did to block the show in the first place, is worth the effort. You're thinking not only about what *you* invent, but more importantly about what the audience invents.

00.17.30 "I was always told that actors don't like it when you operate [camera]. But I've since found out that's not true."

Yeah. Don't always believe what people tell you about how a process has to work, even if they've done more than you, or have more professional standing. They won't always be right. You can't generalise about creative processes.

00.21.06 "You probably expect Sigourney to be the first one to go [to be killed.] But the story is different."

"…but the story is different." Some people like stories that run on rails. We like stories that surprise us.

00.21.35 Big billowing releases of white CO2. "Here we have CO2. Scientists will be asking why have you got all that CO2? I just liked it, so we used it."

"I just liked it, so we used it." Artist prerogative.

00.23.50 "For financial reasons our model wasn't very big, so I filmed it through a home video camera."

Similar moments of invention are revealed through the whole commentary. If they had the resources to make every production element perfect, you wonder whether the film would have been as interesting.

00.26.25 "Jerry [Goldsmith] hit the score with such delicacy – it gives a sense of scale, architecture, civilisation – but not as we know it."

Sound! The emotional effect of music: it changes a space as experienced by a body. [Actually, that last sentence is an approximation of one of Gernot Bohme's theories as discussed in David Toop's book, *Haunted Weather.* We've nicked loads of ideas from that book too.]

00.26.35 Scott says he wants to make a 5th Alien where they go back and find out where the creatures came from; that the crashed spacecraft might be a 'battle carrier', the eggs harbouring some form of biomechanoid warfare.

It's not the idea, it's what you do with it. When we first heard Scott say this back in 2002, it sounded great. Then we saw *Prometheus* in 3D (2012). Hard to believe it's the same director. If you ask me, dude should've taken a good listen to his *Alien* DVD commentary before making *Prometheus*.

00.32.20 *"Those are my hands inside a pair of rubber gloves. Inside a fibreglass case [the translucent eggs]. I always believe if you can do it physically, do it. You could have spent a $100,000 on that effect. It's ridiculous."*

More expensive is not always better. Um… cf. *Prometheus*.

00.36.39 *"The most beautiful technology was in 2001 [A Space Odyssey]. And it was very difficult not to be influenced by that. Tried to avoid it, but inevitably I was influenced by it."*

It's inevitable that you'll be influenced by the things that inspire you. Don't sweat it. Interesting to note how little *Alien* was influenced by *Star Wars*, which was released the year before *Alien* started filming and had such massive popular impact.

00.40.40 *"Using these long shots is good, because it allows the audience to work… It's all about knowing how long you can draw it out before the audience get fidgety."*

Directly influenced: *The Bullet And The Bass Trombone*, where whole sections of the show just involve Tim walking across stage, slowly, whilst unnerving music plays. At every work-in-progress, we asked "are we testing the audience's patience?" But no-one's walked out… yet.

00.49.40 *About asking actors to throw themselves around for effect "You know, whatever it takes. You have to get them [the actors/crew] into that mode where they'll understand that it's all going to be fine."*

Just because you understand what's in your head, doesn't mean anyone else will. So being a good collaborator means making sure people trust you – especially if you're experimenting with things that in theory, sound naff as hell e.g. shakey space vibration acting in 1978.

00.57.20 *"The day that Yaphet had to die, he said, 'I'm not going to die. This thing can't kill me.' So I had to have a long discussion with him persuading him to die that day."*

No matter how much fun you're having, you've got to serve the work. This is harder when you're working in a collaborative or process-driven way e.g. devising. At some point you've got to make decisions about what anchors the work for the audience. Sometimes that means killing Yaphet.

01.02.55 *Dripping water on a spacecraft. "There was a big discussion about this room. Why would you have water in this room? My argument was that it's condensation from the air conditioning."*

We'd never questioned it whilst watching the film. But then, others obviously had. Even though it's not explicit in the film, it's interesting to hear that an internal logic was established to answer those questions. An alternative to the "I just liked it, so we used it" strategy discussed at 00.21.35

01.30.15 *Lambert is killed. "Her death is heard but not seen. Which probably makes it more scary. That was a tough session in the looping stage."*

The story is all told through sound, even though we don't necessarily register that at the time. Don't worry if people don't notice all the clever things you do. The audience don't need to recognise how it's done, to feel the effect of it.

01.30.54 *"I think what we managed to do was put the audience in the position of the person who was about to die. I think we touched on something that makes the audience very vulnerable to what's occurring. Which is why I think it's particularly frightening."*

Image credit: Paul Blakemore

Directly influenced: pretty much everything we do. It's difficult, whilst doing all the logistical stuff that feeds a working process, to keep thinking about what it feels like to dive into the act of imagination anew. This is a reminder to keep thinking how best to invite the audience into the experience. Sometimes our shows ask a question directly *(Astronaut,)* sometimes it's about inviting the audience into the gaps between specific details *(The Dead Phone,)* sometimes it's about physical relationship *(SUPERNOVA.)*

01.37.40 "Here's where we're all heading towards the end of the movie. And I felt the film could not end here. But there was a big battle about 'this is it. The film's over,' I felt: the rhythm is wrong, 'Cos after all, rhythm's the music. The music of the story is wrong. You can't end the film here. It's not that simple. Because for her to shoot in, sit in the seat, take off – just didn't make sense. So there was a big play of what to do, I knew what to do. And said the Alien has to be in this craft – so it's like the fourth act. They felt it was overkill. And I said, really you need overkill. In a film like this, you need overkill. And in fact I think in recent years, films have come up with endings on endings on endings."

It *felt* wrong to the end the film here. The *music of the story* made it wrong to end there – not the theory, or the plotting, but *the music* of the story. When you know the film, it's crazy to think they might have ended it at this point. We use this idea of musicality as a dramaturgical tool all the time. It's more than just: does it make sense? It's also about: does it feel right? Do the dissonances and harmonies make for a rich experience?

01.51.18 "When you put a good bunch of people together it becomes all very inspirational. And I think above all things, if it's not fun, you shouldn't be doing it."

POOL RULES

DO NOT:

- AVOID SWEATING
- WORK, LIVE AND CREATE THEATRE WITH THE SAME PEOPLE
- GET COMFORTABLE
- RELY ON A TECHNICIAN
- LET YOUR AUDIENCE GET ATTACHED

DO:

- KEEP ARMS AND LEGS ON STAGE AT ALL TIMES
- LEARN FROM YOUR LAST SHOW
- WARM UP
- PERFORM ANYWHERE
- USE YOURSELF AND OTHERS

REPORT ANY INCIDENTS OR UNSAFE CONDITIONS TO MANAGEMENT IMMEDIATELY.
WE PROBABLY WON'T DO ANYTHING ABOUT IT BUT THANKS FOR TELLING US.

POOL HOURS
8:00 AM - DUSK

SLEEPING TREES

DO NOT:

Avoid Sweating - We sweat, a lot. If we aren't sweating buckets on stage, we don't feel like we've put on a good show. We believe that if your audience are to take anything from a performance it should at least be a face full of salty sweat to show how hard you've worked; that way, at least your enthusiasm is safe from scrutiny.

Work, Live & Create Theatre With The Same People - We have been living together on and off for four years, and have just put down a deposit on a new house to move in together again. Living together means a lot of time in the rehearsal space is saved because we have already discussed all our ideas at home over reheated lasagna. The down side is it becomes very easy to become caught up in your own world and needless arguments are unavoidable; in these times, an outside eye is key for us.

Get Comfortable - Doing the same show again and again means it can become very easy to get comfortable. As soon as we know a show well enough to become completely comfortable performing it, we begin to change it. Adding in new lines and trying to catch each other out off guard helps keep the work fresh for both our audience and us.

Rely On A Technician - We feel like we should be able to get up and go straight away with a performance. We require nothing more than a standard lighting wash from a technician and there have been some situations where even that has let us down. The less we need from other people the more we can just blame each other if anything goes wrong.

Let Your Audience Get Attached - In the same way we keep each other on our toes, we don't like our audience to become too settled either. Nothing brings us more joy than taking an audience on a journey with a character only to have brutally slaughtered at the final hurdle and leave our audience searching for something else or mildly depressed.

DO:

Keep Arms & Legs Onstage At All Times - We don't like to be off stage, unless its necessary, at the same time you don't want to stand on stage doing nothing. It's at these moments we find ourselves being most creative through the devising process.

Learn From Your Last Show - We are never afraid to cut and change as we go. The writing of a show doesn't have to stop just because the tour has begun, every audience we perform to provides us with fresh feedback with which to develop the show.

Warm Up - We have learnt the hard way about not warming up before a show. Numerous days in bed with aches and pains, which, if you're on tour means you just to have to suck it up and lump it. So seriously, warm up.

Perform Anywhere - We have done some weird shows in the past, in some weird locations. The most recent of which was a full hour-long performance in front of the only toilets in a Brick Lane curry house as well as performing to a crèche of three year olds in a cafe to due to a slight administrative error on our behalf. But each odd gig provides a new challenge and a new opportunity to change and challenge us as performers.

Use Yourself & Others - We learnt very quickly that you can't be afraid to get up, close and personal with each other. We have locked lips, licked faces, put fingers down throats, climbed over, under and through each other on stage. If we did not commit to such intimate physical exchanges, the audience may not deem them necessary to the performance, as well as just being a bit concerned for the well being of everyone involved.

OR, ALL YOU NEED TO MAKE A SHOW IS A GIRL AND A MICROPHONE

For us, DIY was never so much about ideology or even economic necessity as it was about having complete and absolute and actually-on-reflection-basically-megalomanic creative control over every aspect of our work; about never really having to explain or justify ourselves to anybody; about limiting our work to what was or wasn't inside of our own heads and nobody else's – little proper technique in any of this, little if any research, just what we remembered and liked from the lives we lived and the films we saw. Any skills we didn't already have or couldn't teach ourselves with the minimum of effort and at least a little fun we just kind of ignored.

"For whom is the Funhouse fun?"
John Barth, *Lost In The Funhouse.*

If the live act is good for *anything* it's pulling the language of the modern world – all billboards and jingles and over-lit desire – out into the open: ripping it out of context, wilfully misinterpreting it, making it too real or not real enough. There's something transformative about taking that language into a room in front of strangers and *looking them in the eye whilst you're speaking*, as if the voice with which the world speaks to us (*at* us, deafeningly, day and night) starts speaking in tongues, speaking back to itself, echoes and reflects off as if down a hall of mirrors. And once detached from "reality" it becomes suddenly something sensual, something warm and tactile, a fake that's even better than the real thing. If there's *fun* inside any of this it's probably here, this thing. There is perhaps some kind of moral and/or political dimension to all this but we've never been much interested. And at it's best (in the giddy peaks of Action Hero's *Watch Me Fall*, in Sanja Mitrovic's extraordinary *Will You Ever Be Happy Again?*) there's a sense not of rupture or of refusal but rather of this language actually somehow resolving itself, becoming music, finding the melody line it's been feeling for, falling for an all-too-brief moment into perfect harmony or awful clarity, until the show ends and the doors open and the world comes flooding back in again.

SHOWS (1)

Most of our shows start out, at the very beginning of development, with some kind of mechanism that will hopefully throw up enough dramatic possibilities to carry us through the initial devising stages and which should, if it works, pull both us and the audience through the finished show; these structures are usually "borrowed" from the outside world – as for example in Karaoke *(2013) the karaoke machine that's feeding us all of our text and actions throughout the show – in order simultaneously to drive the show's structure and to locate the thing inside a broader cultural context. Text, action, music, projection, etc, are all developed parallel to each other, with all the different parts hopefully speaking to and informing each other along the way. We nowadays make all of the music and projections for our shows ourselves, on the same aging laptop these words were written on, making our own audio and video samples with a microphone and a toy guitar and a camcorder, chopping and looping and filtering everything until it feels for whatever reason "right", alive. Music particularly has become so integral to structure that we'll sometimes score and sequence it before text and action, which will then be layered on top according to whatever tone the music's setting, whoever's voice sits best inside of it, etc. Done right, this gives us the space to stick more or less whatever we want into the show with the musical structure there as a kind of safety net, holding everything together and keeping it moving. Most of the rest of the process is just following hunches, threads, vague suspicions. We don't usually find out what the show is about until we've almost finished making it. Generally it takes us 18 months to completely finish a show, enough time to make two babies.*

PERFECT SHOW

The perfect show always in our heads, the show we're always heading towards, is the show where *nothing happens* – without performers, without a theatre, without an audience, without time passing, without anything in it at all, just absolute stillness, absolute darkness, absolute silence. Every performance we've ever made has been a movement towards this perfect zero point; every score we've ever constructed has included the instruction "do nothing"; the task has always been to do things slower, quieter, with less feeling, less expression. There is something that happens to a face when all of the expression is pulled out of it; stare long enough into an empty face and your imagination starts to fill it up with *everything*; listen long enough to an empty voice and you'll just fall into it. And then also the closer you get to zero the more everything that's left – the tiniest gesture, the slightest break in the voice, the vaguest hint of a smile – just kind of *vibrates* with life. (People sometimes ask us why we always use microphones and it's for this – to capture every whisper, every breath). And it's like once the noise and distractions are removed you can grasp, finally, what it is you were really looking at all along.

SHOWS (2)

Sometimes we think of our shows as really films that we have to stage over and over again because we don't know how to film them. Sometimes we think of our shows as really novels that we have to draft over and over because we don't know how to finish them. Sometimes we think of our shows as really songs with no singing in them.

"For whom is the Funhouse a house?"
David Foster Wallace, *Westward The Course Of Empire Takes Its Way.*

And all the time more than anything we've been trying to hear what our own voices sound like, to hear what kind of things those voices should be saying, are *already* somehow saying, somewhere just beyond hearing. We've been trying to catch the expressions that our faces seem already to be hiding, the gestures our bodies want to make, the thoughts we can't stop thinking. If we've ever learnt anything it has been how to understand ourselves as materials, in a tactile and physical rather than psychological or autobiographical sense; to look not for "inner truth" (and anyway we've always preferred lying) but for the stuff that's seems to be already kind of latent, written into the surface, the only part of us that will ever anyway be visible to the audience. All you need to make a show is a girl and a microphone; you just need to figure out what she looks like she's about to say. This is all, perhaps, something like looking at the cover of a book and imagining what kind of story you'd most *like* to find inside it, and then trying to write that one. By now we know, more-or-less, the different versions of each other that we'd most like to write. We've known each other for ten years and worked together for most of that. We can't remember anymore who else we might have become, or were to begin with. We've known each other forever. And if we've never quite understood, really and truthfully, what it is that we're doing – always lagging somehow behind, always running to catch up with the thought, the moment, each other – we know at least that we *Did It Ourselves*, that the blood is on our hands, that we are ourselves woven inside of every show, whether we like it or not, inseparable.

HOMEWORK

Which movements best resemble stillness? Which sounds best resemble silence? Which ideas best resemble nothing? Which people best resemble nobody?

END

We've always loved making the endings. The ending is always the best bit. A good ending is both a farewell and also a kind of latching on, the show crawling into the heads of the audience like a shiver of longing, like a tickle of doubt, like a parasite. A good ending is a kind of epiphany, like in the dying moments you can suddenly catch sight of the whole thing, of what it really was, the show, and in that glimpsing it all twist back in on itself, like an impossible, unmappable funhouse, dizzying, serpentine, exitless. It never ends. It always ends. It ends all too suddenly ...

Being able to Do It Yourself was one of theatre's major lures. Back in the (very) late '80s doing film yourself seemed highly unlikely and theatre had what it will always have, the kid's from *Fame!* let's-do-the-show-right-here-in-the-canteen possibility. We could do theatre ourselves so we did do theatre ourselves. Graeme Rose and I formed Stan's Cafe.

One of the things we noticed doing theatre ourselves in those early days was that we weren't always by ourselves, an audience often tagged along with us. Not only did they tag along but they seemed eager to help us in the doing.

We reflected on our own responses to watching theatre and recognised that the shows we hated most were those in which the company did it all themselves: the working things out and connection making, the thinking and emoting. Out in the audience we wanted to do some of that ourselves. As a result in Stan's Cafe shows we started to leave the audience with work to do: resonances to trace back, references to hunt down, ghosts to divine, rules to decode. Like most DIY jobs our shows were left unfinished – not without an end but consistently unfinished throughout, needing more work doing by the audience moment to moment.

In 1998, after an extended apprenticeship, we gave our audience a promotion. For the first time they didn't just help 'finish' the show, they stared in it. The optical tricks *It's Your Film* is built around demand it be watched by a single audience member. As the audience member watches through a rectangular aperture from a small wooden viewing booth 270 seconds of narrative unfold with alternating, cross-fading images of a detective and a lover searching the city for someone. As the action reaches a finale the two hunters' images dissolve into each other only to be replaced by the audience's own reflection and a rear projection that frames them as the missing third protagonist, the hunted 'other' who has escaped and is in a cab at night travelling through the rain. This final scene is all theirs, just by sitting watching the drama they find themselves in the drama, doing it themselves.

STAN'S CAFE
& AUDIENCE DIY

The audience DIY required in *The Black Maze* (2000-10) is more active. Neatly described as 'a ghost train without the train' this series of narrow, pitch-black corridors with hidden doors and sensory effects was designed to be walked through by its audience. Inspired by the notion that those monsters hidden in the dark of a labyrinth may merely be projections of the psyche of whoever is inside, the audience are ideally left to journey through the maze alone responding to events they unwittingly trigger themselves as they travel.

On their first journey through/performance of *The Black Maze* audiences tended to report a fixation on narrative resolution; can they (the protagonist) escape unharmed? Their spontaneous cries and bumps, audible from outside the maze, turn those awaiting their journey into a de facto audience, heightening anticipation for the moment they will step up to perform. On subsequent journeys, with the set/narrative mechanics now known, audiences report savouring their performance more, being less focused on reaching its conclusion and more playful with the content. They grow more confident in their role and start to enjoy it, choosing where to linger and when to move on. They no longer cry out, they are now performing purely for themselves, simultaneously actor and audience: doing it for themselves.

In *The Steps Series* (2008 – present) audiences are also expected to act but the drama is more conventional and both script and blocking instructions are far more proscribed. Audiences follow trails of footprints and handprints, speech bubbles and 'object prints' stuck across arts venues / shopping centres / streets in brightly coloured vinyl and are encouraged to physically place themselves in the action and by so doing puzzle out the actions that are encoded in the vinyl. Like playwrights we leave once our vinyl script/text/notation is stuck and now the audience DIY extends to direction as well as acting. Now they must cast each other, study the 'text', rehearse the actions and speech before performing a 'best' version, they are free to skip scenes, re-cast, extend, approximate and improvise.

These three productions take the idea of audiences doing it themselves to progressively more extreme levels, with the company steadily withdrawing from the scene of the action. The audience moves from being heavily framed as a performer by the show's action, to performing for themselves in a private drama, to attempting more conventional acting under their own direction from a 'script' we have left behind. These pieces are spread over a period of ten years and are interspersed with numerous other productions in which the audience DIY aesthetic is explored in more subtle and conceptual ways. Binding all these shows together is a belief that audiences should be allowed to do some work on the shows themselves, it is however important to recognise that we do not abdicate responsibility to audiences. We are the people with the originating vision, aptitude, training and experience. Audiences are required to Do It Themselves in Stan's Cafe shows but we'd still like to help out occasionally.

Main image: Ed Dimsdale
Image below: BeBe Jacobs courtesy of Skirball Cultural Center

Now, inevitably, it's your turn. Here's how to establish your own International Airport:

Be reckless and just get on with it. Make it hard to be easily defined (by choosing an impossible name). Resist any attempts to say what you do or might do in the future (this will scupper your chances of funding, but that's OK), don't strive to be at all well known - so no pandering to journalists or trying to get in Time Out (this will also help with avoiding the law). Don't worry if at first you don't know what you're doing or what you want, embrace the principle of the chisel [5] and get going on defining what you don't want.

Care for those you work with, trust them. Feel love and don't be afraid to admit it. Put everything you have into the project - the personality is as important as the concept. Any sort of directorship, artistic or otherwise is like high-speed gardening, you must be present and attentive.

Avoid making any concessions to the utterly horrid system we operate in. Do not engage in various cultural-capital building exercises such as carefully selecting who performs or working hard on a set statement or brand. Be so in-the-moment with everything that it drags others in, they will be enthused by your energy and what appears to be total disregard for future problems. Let others get scared about that if they want to. Be as open, inclusive and altruistic as possible, become a place beyond criticism in that it stands for nothing but the fact it is possible to create something whose only ambition is to exist as an example of such a thing. People will hardly believe it's real.

Dogs in Yachts [5]

So, a working philosophy (which is also a metaphor because I'm a sloppy writer) could be - take the hot potato from the oven, give it to someone and say, ok, your go, whatever you do is fine (the hotness of the potato will prevent stasis). This may sound totally unserious and irresponsible but its a very good way to make things happen. The fact that I do not control what comes next is not to be seen as deserting my obligations as an artist, rather, accepting that all eventualities that flow from a significant moment are entrained in the artistic impulse with which that moment is given. It's playful, dangerous and not always successful, but if I wanted to see ratifiable success, I'd be a cleaner.

(1) The world's first mini-festival of one-on-one performance
(2) Beckett, *Waiting for Godot*
(3) Orlagh Woods asked this during a meeting to organise the wake for New Work Network
(4) Harrison Owen, inventor of Open Space, the system that Devoted and Disgruntled uses
(5) You read it here first
(6) A suggestion for Gary Campbell's contribution which didn't make his cut

<u>Sui generis</u>

Stoke Newington International Airport is and was the kind of place we wished existed, where you do something that you like and let someone else do something that they like. It was payback to all those who have let me (or us, or you) use a space for free - who had done it themselves before us. From March 2008 to April 2013 we produced a performance event every month alongside inventing Live Art Speed Date[1], and making the space available for anyone that wanted to use it. We were gleefully hands off too: You want to use the space, do. You want the stage moved or lights rigged? do it yourself. Not many people did the cleaning themselves though, we did that. I did a lot of thinking while mopping the floor.

<u>There's no lack of void</u> [2]

Way before STK, the first proper show I made was a lecture performance called How to Build a Time Machine. In his shed, a father builds a time machine from cardboard, wire and a fuse box in the hope of preventing the death of his daughter. He speaks to us, and to her and to you. He tells us "everything is connected, we are all connected" while slipping a noose of wire around the necks of the audience. I wanted them and still want them to wake up from their dream of reality. DIY may well be an aesthetic, a wave, or a phase, but I'm only interested in shouting "Do It Yourself!" as an imperative for action.

We all have an artist in the dark back of the brain, a suspension of ideas, missions, actions, and decisions which only come through as sparks in dreams or strange desires in awkward moments. These impulses flow in movement, discussion, with an instrument, or when time is extremely tight, literally seconds before something must be said or done. So my process (at least for now) is to create an environment where this flow can happen. This generally begins with getting someone else to goad me into action (because I cannot do it myself) and in turn, I become the goad, and so on.

<u>You guys don't play the game, do you?</u> [3]

STK was always we. When I found the space I felt the thrill of knowing it required a group. There is now a famous judgment-within-a-maxim: Whoever comes are the right people[4]. And they were. And they continued to be. The practical realisation of STK was almost impossible without the continuous support of others. We gave anyone that wanted it a taste of the 'underground', the explicit message being "your help means we don't have to ask for any". For the helpers, contributors, performers and punters, there was varying benefit from their involvement, but each of them can quite honestly and proudly say that if not for them STK could not have survived. That, if anything, was the radical element of the project - that it existed at all.

DILUTE INVOLUNTARY

DISTRUST ILL YOLKS

DEVISE IDENTITY YEARL

DIVULGE INTERNET YEA

DON'T INJURE YOURSE

DISOBEY INWARD YAW

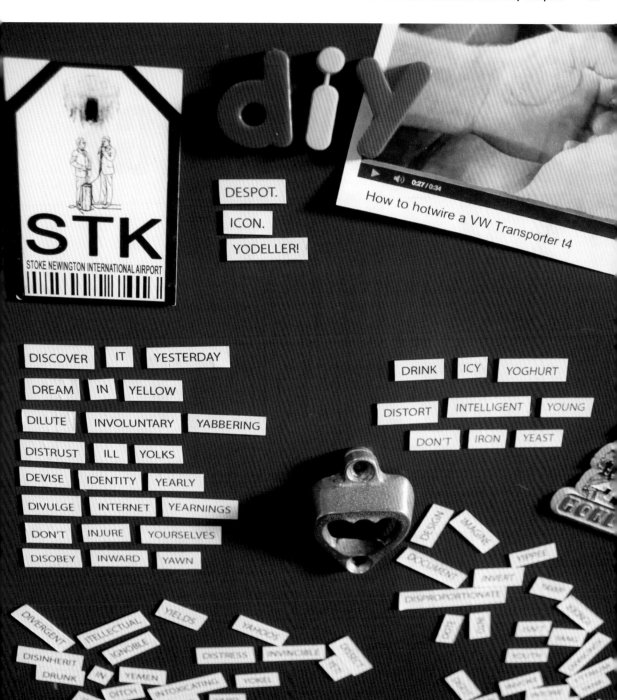

WHEN YOU WALK ONSTAGE TONIGHT TO BRING THE NOISE, TREAT IT LIKE IT'S ALL WE HAVE.

Bruce Springsteen, SXSW Keynote Speech, 15/3/12

This is a letter to people starting out and wanting to make DIY theatre. Wanting to know what it feels like to make DIY theatre. A letter in which I can share with you my experience of what DIY theatre is, has been, and should be. I hope there is at least one sentence here to kick-start your own development.

DIY THEATRE IS

- being electrocuted more than once.
- filling your studio with junk and trying everything, until that room is only full of *essential* junk.
- wiring your CD player that you got when you were 16 to the onstage sound desk.
- turning a paint shop into a venue.
- the most exciting way of making theatre.
- building the set to the dimension of your car so that you can drive your show to the next town. To any town.
- playing an impromptu music set to an audience because midway through the show your CD player that you got when you were 16 burnt out and now your mate has to run five blocks away to get a replacement.
- the hardest and most rewarding way to make theatre.
- making new friends: battery operated lights, household lamps, extension cords, cable ties, gaffa, hot glue guns, cardboard, car speakers. These are your friends now.
- driving through the night, unpacking a show, setting it up, delivering your all, packing it up and driving onward to do it all again, just the same but different every time.
- having a drill on stage incase any of the set falls apart mid show.
- fostering relationships with people, theatres and Universities who are willing to champion your work and support your development. These relationships are so important to your company's longevity.
- shutting down a whole docklands site because you were performing in a shipping container and cut through mains power with a cleaver. Should have used a prop cleaver.
- ripping off set designs that you saw in main stage theatres and re-designing them with $500.
- creating an environment where the audience and you are complicit.
- having theatre programmers not take you seriously, and learning not to take it personally but use it as fuel to win them over.
- thinking OFF the grid. (The Suitcase Royale used motorbike batteries to power our latest show, *Zombatland*. This was conceptually effective since the show is set in a low-budget caravan park, and saved cash and time as those batteries are rechargeable too. During one of our seasons the theatre lost power and we were the only production still able to run that night.)

- inviting your heroes to see your work. (Bruce Springsteen is invited to each season of The Suitcase Royale's work.)
- saying "what's that buzz" 1 minute before your first sold out audience is about to enter.
- building a community and network of artists from all over the world.
- fixing "that buzz" 20 seconds before your first sold out audience is about to enter.
- researching different council's throw out days and driving through the suburbs collecting other peoples junk to build into your set. Old Home Entertainment speakers, fittings, leather suitcases, household lamps: other peoples cast-offs have become The Suitcase Royale's props and sets for years.
- sharing beers with the audience after a show and getting feedback directly from them.
- late night gigs with musicians from all over the world.
- having reviewers not understand you because they can't pigeonhole your work: "are they are band? A theatre company? A comedy troupe? A bunch of amateurs?" [1]
- selling beers at the show to fund your petrol money while on tour.
- learning how to wire together your own lighting rig.
- booking your own tours and thinking outside the box as to where you can perform.
- learning how to use spreadsheets.
- having an audience member come up to you on the street and hand you a brand new replica prop. They were in the show last night when you broke the original.
- making music, writing music and recording music. Being a band.
- becoming your own lighting designer, operator, actor, set designer and musician. Take the time and effort to acquire technical skills. The more self-contained you are when you are first starting out the more you can make and tour.
- having a Chihuahua run on stage mid-show, because the Chihuahua lives in the space where you are performing. Then making the Chihuahua star of the next scene.
- multi-tasking. (In our shows the lighting desk is usually by my drum-kit. I hold the sticks in my mouth or drum one-handed when I need to change the lighting state.)
- sacrificing summer to make a great show in a black box.
- making more from less (cash). Production values don't make a show. It comes down to sweat and craft. Having no money can be the best thing for a production because it forces you to find ways of building the grand images from nothing.
- OK if it's accessible.
- a party that you initiate, where everyone is in the space together for this small time and what ever happens on that particular night only happens on that night.
- stealing from every artform.
- doing it yourself – in which 'it' is everything. Not just the creative but also the practical. Be your own producer, treasurer, grant-writer, driver, and PR. And anything else you need to make the art and give it to its audience.

Reference
[1] Guardian online article *"Is this amateur night"*:
http://www.theguardian.com/stage/2011/aug/10/edinburgh-comedy-notebook-amateur-bungling

DIY THEATRE IS TREATING IT LIKE IT'S ALL YOU HAVE, AND THEN BRINGING THE NOISE

Joseph O'Farrell (JOF)

DIY(s): SHARE ▷ Collaborate

I do it myself – You do it yourself –
They do it themselves – we do it ourselves.

DIY is good because it's the way *you* do it. It's personal. Some people take personal-ness to mean small-ness; and some people equate small-ness to trivial, insubstantial, inconsequential.. Alternatively, you could consider the personal to be the stuff that matters most: the heart and soul.

Theatre Bristol emerged in response to what was happening in Bristol around a decade ago – and what was happening was a groundswell of strong independent performance being made in the city, and increasingly touring out of the city. This was in 2004, and that groundswell was largely centred around, on the one hand, a very active street arts community and on the other, an experimental performance community nurtured by Arnolfini's live art and dance programme. In short, this was not mainstream. This was alternative. This was artist-led. This was DIY.

It's the personal that makes DIY practice so important to a healthy creative community. Whether through punk or folk or bloodymindedness or accident, it's the personal drive of DIY practice that keeps it plural, meaningful, subversive.

When you look at Bristol in 2013, it looks like independent, personally-driven artistic practice is embraced as a matter of course. Artist-led collectives like Residence, Interval and Puppet Place are firmly part of an ecology that supports artists of international standing; the singular vision of In Between Time is established as an Arts Council national portfolio organisation; Mayfest, 10 years old now, is led by two producers, who moved out of an institution to deliver a festival of increasing scale and renown, with no regular funding, working out of a temporary office in a disused shop; even Bristol Old Vic – the biggy – is regularly platforming and commissioning work by independent artists.

What happened in between, and what Theatre Bristol was instrumental to, was the fostering of a culture of conversation, generosity and sharing that helped break down hierarchies and give independent voices more space to be heard in the same rooms as the institutions. You could call it networking. You could call it getting to know each other. But it led to more confidence, less suspicion, more interest in this city from artists and others, and much more prevalence of the word 'community' in relation to the people involved in making art here.

I'm not sure if it's cool to admit it, but I think this is a good thing. I think it's a good thing that the resources and profile normally restricted to major institutions are being connected to more independent artists and producers. I think it's a good thing that electing to work independently does not necessarily mean working without infrastructure.

But then, if DIY is personal, how do you keep it DIY when you're working with an institution: an entity, a *thing* that by its very structure is *im*personal? Should we be challenging those institutions to come out from behind their policies and get more personal?

Theatre Bristol is an organisation. And we're also a group of people. We can be personal, and collective. Do it yourself. Do it yourselves. Do it together.

INFILTRATE

Here are some options:
- Be completely honest with each other
- Share stuff properly – not in the sense of 'you can share access to our database for a small fee', but in the sense of 'the building's open anyway and no-one's using that space, so of course you can use it', or 'this is the ENTIRE budget relating to the project, including all the staff and building costs; shall we look together at what we can cut, so that we can pay you an appropriate fee?'
- Believe that a successful collaboration is where your collaborator gets more from it than you do.
- Get to know each other. Eat together. Everyone. Not just the arty types, but also the finance types and the technician types and the audience types.
- Remember the audience are people.
- Remember the artists are people.
- Remember the staff are people.
- Stop talking about brand.
- Don't talk about creditation.
- Talk about ethics.
- Talk about bands.
- Talk about love.
- Talk about art.
- Do it differently.
- Treat the institution like a person, until it treats you back with the same degree of friendship / high-quality conversation / "humorous" joshing / emotional commitment / respect.
- Don't take the money.

Links to the other groups / organisations / institutions mentioned: Arnolfini (arnolfini.org.uk), Residence (residence.org.uk), Interval (intervalbristol.org), Puppet Place (puppetplace.org), In Between Time (inbetweentime.co.uk), Mayfest (mayfestbristol.co.uk), Bristol Old Vic (bristololdvic.org.uk), Theatre Bristol (theatrebristol.net).

Poster on reverse

BEWARE THE SOFA

In Third Angel we have a saying: *Beware The Sofa*. To be honest we have quite a few sayings, just because we've been working together so long. A verbal short hand to help move things on. We've learned over the years, for example, that it can be tempting, when involved in an exciting discussion about the work you're making, to re-explain something someone else has already said that you like, but in your own words. So we taught ourselves to say "I agree." Sounds obvious I know, but it took a bit of doing. And it's the attractiveness of this sitting and talking that "Beware The Sofa" is designed to guard against.

Talking about ideas is really important. Bouncing those ideas off each other, sending them off at tangents, watching the sparks fly. It can feel like the best bit of making work. Sitting talking. Someone's brought some good coffee in, and some nice speciality biscuits. Oh, and are those fresh grapes? Suddenly it's lunchtime, and an hour later the day resumes with cups of tea and a recap, and actually this sofa is pretty comfy for lying on, isn't it, and actually us having a chat about something not really related to the show is good for the group dynamic. What we could do, is stay here and just get a really good plan together for tomorrow, and try some stuff out first thing...

If we've learned anything about making work, it's that whilst the talking, and imagining, is brilliant and important, at some point you have to get up and do something. To see if what you're talking about is interesting, is what you think it is. If you're all talking about the same thing, in fact. Because even if you don't like it, even if it doesn't work, then you've got something shared, and specific, to say "not that" about. And if it is working, then you've got something to build on, to evolve from.

Because, almost definitely, something will have happened differently in practice to what you were expecting. So you have something to respond to, together. Something that happened, not just in your imagination, but in the room.

BEWARE THE SOFA

'The best ever death metal band out of Denton were a couple of guys who'd been friends since grade school one was named Cyrus the other was Jeff and they practiced twice a week in Jeff's bedroom.'

The Best Ever Death Metal Band Out Of Denton - track 2 on All Hail West Texas, by the Mountain Goats.

Cyrus and Jeff's story in the rest of that song isn't a happy one. Societal disapproval of Jeff and Cyrus's shared ideals means Cyrus gets sent to a school that crushes his dreams of metal stardom, and Jeff... well at the end of the song, Jeff's writing letters to Cyrus about an unspecified plan to 'get even' and you kind of know it isn't going to end well. Have a listen to that song now. It's on youtube. Everything's on youtube.

It's a beautiful song. It's about how conservative communities destroy difference, and it's about being a rock star, and it's about the joy of making something worthwhile with your best friends, and the final chorus (if you haven't listened to it yet, it's just 'Hail Satan' repeated a few times over the main chord progression) is a defiant fuck you from two young men who got sick of being told they were evil.

And of course it's about the tape-hiss. The hiss is all over it. Not part of the melodic structure of the song, carrying no meaning or sentiment. Getting in the way when you first hear it. But absolutely what makes it work. A relic of the fact it was played and sung into a Panasonic RX-FT500 boombox with a single condenser microphone. But the tape-hiss is what makes it. It wraps it all up in defiance, but it's also the structural core of the song. It's the tape-hiss of a million bedroom bands, and it's the jarring, fractured noise of the world with the truth shining through it.

John Darnielle of the Mountain Goats is one of the greatest DIY artists of his or any other generation. Even though the albums that came after All Hail West Texas were recorded in studios, even though there's orchestration, and arrangement, and clarity, the hiss is still there. There might be drums, and overdubs, and synthesised sounds. But when he was recording the first few albums on the RX-FT500, he swallowed the hiss, and it still comes out through the cracks in his voice.

The hiss is the sound of working things out. It's the background hum of the Universe. It's the hair on the lens. It's microwaves. It's dark matter and it's gamma-ray-bursts and it's the other sounds in the room. It doesn't have to be audible, but it's there. It's a fundamental result of you being here. Whether you acknowledge it or not is up to you.

All Hail Cyrus and Jeff.

BIOGRAPHIES
of contributors

ROBERT DANIELS

Robert is an interdisciplinary artist and teacher. He is a founder and co-Artistic Director of Bootworks Theatre, and a Senior Lecturer in Theatre at The University of Chichester. His specialisms include: UK-centric Performance Studies, Practice as Research, Live Art, Interdisciplinary Performance, Dance Theatre, Street Theatre and Site Specific Art, and devised theatre performance. Independent projects include *Tiny Live Art* (supported by The ShowRoom Theatre, Chichester and Forest Fringe), *Playing with MySelf* (2003) (ACE funded and supported by The Battersea Arts Centre) and scorezer0, (ACE funded and supported by RALP funded Choreographic Lab). Other work includes collaborations with Jane Bacon (and red leaf dance videos) on two entries for the Video Place's One Minute Wander dance video competition (winners 2000), premiered at Cinemarket 2001 by the Danish film institute and Bodyworks 2001 festival in Melbourne. Robert is a graduate of The University of Northampton (BA) and University of Kent (MA). Over the years Robert has also collaborated with and trained with a number of artists, including Sally Dean, Trestle, New Art Club, Nicolas Nunez, Libby Worth and Helen Poyner, The New World Performance Laboratory, Goat Island, Xavier Le Roy, Mary Overlie, and V-Tol dance.

• www.bootworkstheatre.co.uk
• www.chiuni.ac.uk/theatre
• @robjudedaniels

ACCIDENTAL COLLECTIVE: Pablo Pakula and Daisy Orton

We are Accidental Collective, an interdisciplinary performance company based in Kent. With our roots in theatre and live art, we create innovative work that engages with people and places. We have created outdoor performances, theatre shows, one-to-one encounters, participatory installations, immersive experiences, and public interventions. We are drawn to notions of fragmentation, encounter, and multiplicity. Our work is generous, participatory and visually striking - it has both a big heart and a strong mind. As the performance scene in Kent has gradually grown, we have offered peer support and mentoring to other performers and companies. In 2011 this led us to establish a performance-sharing platform: Pot Luck. This is part and parcel of Accidental Collective's ethos, and links back to our work: a process informed by connection, conversation and collaboration. Accidental Collective is Daisy Orton and Pablo Pakula. We like strong coffee, small beautiful things, mind-boggling Postmodern theory, watching BBC4 documentaries and crap American dramas, rummaging through attics, discovering new places, and having a really good cry. We also like lists. When not being Accidental Collective, we also teach at the University of Kent.

• www.accidentalcollective.co.uk
• @accidentalC
• @PotLuckKent

ACTION HERO: James Stenhouse and Gemma Paintin

We live and work in Bristol where we have been making performance together since 2005. We make performance, live art and theatre that is interested in pop cultural mythologies and the creation of temporary communities centred around the live event. Our work often has a sense of the epic, even though it is played out through a lo-fi, DIY approach to performance-making.

• www.actionhero.org.uk
• @Actionherolive

ARNOLFINI: Liz Clarke

Liz Clarke is a live artist and performer. Practicing in the spaces between theatre, cabaret and live art she questions what happens when the genres' unwritten rules are broken, merged, unclassified, exploited. Her work is strongly connected with representing the Female through alienation, intimacy and construction of mythical Hyperfeminine archetypes. She has performed UK wide on stages, understairs, cars, in giant balloons & clubs UK wide, including In between Time, Arnolfini, Duckie, Roundhouse, Shunt, PerformanceSpace and Mayfest, She is part of the performance collective 'Residence' and artistic director of Drastic Productions. Arnolfini is a Space For Ideas. In a fantastic waterside location at the heart of Bristol's harbourside, Arnolfini is one of Europe's leading centres for the contemporary arts, presenting innovative, experimental work in the visual arts, performance, dance, film, music and events, accompanied by a programme of educational activities. Five exhibition spaces, a theatre/cinema auditorium, Reading Room and Light/Dark Studios are housed in the Grade II listed, fully accessible building. The converted warehouse also contains one of the country's best arts bookshops as well as a café bar serving the best in local and seasonal produce. Arnolfini is a registered charity, core funded by Arts Council England and in receipt of regular funding from Bristol City Council.

- www.arnolfini.org.uk
- @ArnolfiniArts
- @LizGClarke

PAT ASHE

Pat Ashe is a performance maker, live artist and games designer. His work blends genres, mediums and forms and has been shown at a variety of contexts. He runs Beta Public, a night for videogames and theatre designed to explore what the two mediums have in common. He is a founder member of How We Run, a performance collective of live artists and academics whose work focuses on the gap between audience and artist. He used to run We Want Your Dog, a performance night based in Winchester, showcasing both local and national talent.

- www.thepatashe.wordpress.com
- @patrickashe

BOOTWORKS: James Baker and Andy Roberts

Bootworks Theatre Collective is James Baker, Robert Jude Daniels, Andy Roberts, producer Becki Haines and associate artists Natalie Green, Daniel Kok and Sophia Walls. We are a group of artists who work in a range of disciplines and contexts. We make a varied spectrum of work from children's shows to live art, street theatre and devised performance. A lot of our work is driven by a desire to bring unusual theatre and performance to unconventional audiences. Bootworks are resident artists at the ShowRoom Theatre, Chichester. James Baker is a theatre maker, academic and artist. Recent projects have been focusing upon the relationship between travel and performance; looking particularly at how the experience of travel can be documented through the act of performing. *30 Days to Space* and *30 Days to Edinburgh* have both been works that attempt to explore the conceptual nature of travel and present the beginning of a continued engagement with this research agenda. James is an Associate Lecturer in the Theatre Department at the University of Chichester. Previously he has taught on the undergraduate programme at The University of Portsmouth and guest lectured on the M.A in Advanced Theatre Practice at RCSSD. He has been published in numerous publications and has won a Total Theatre Award for Innovation in 2010. Andy Roberts is a Theatre maker and one of the three Artistic Directors of Bootworks Theatre. He is also the programmer for the ShowRoom Theatre Chichester. Andy joined Bootworks Theatre in 2006 and became a joint Artistic Director of the company in 2011. Since 2006 Andy as contributed to all Bootworks projects in some shape or form and has had a great time doing it. Andy has created two solo works alongside the company, Predator finishing off what I started when I was five and Now listen to me very carefully as well as leading on rural touring and intern projects with The Black Box project *The Good the Bad and the Box*. Andy is also founding member of Play Possum Theatre (2007) with Natalie Evans, and Pinchmil Theatre (2009) with Mark Newnham, and has occasionally written for Total theatre

Magazine (2011) Andy has a BA Hons in Performing Arts as well as a MA in Theatre Collectives. He currently resides in Chichester as he doesn't feel he's cool enough to live in Brighton or London, but enjoys a good visit from time to time.

- www.bootworkstheatre.co.uk
- @bootworks

IRA BRAND

Ira is an artist, performance-maker and writer, working across theatre and live art. Her practice is rooted in the experience of being human, rather than in singular narratives, and strives to make an audience re- consider themselves, and the world within which they live, through work that is evocative and intimate. Ira was a founding member of collaborative performance group Tinned Fingers, and regularly works in collaboration with other companies and artists, which have included People Show, Living Structures, Made In China and Andy Field. She is Associate Producer for Forest Fringe.

- www.irabrand.co.uk
- @irabrand

KAREN CHRISTOPHER

Karen Christopher is a collaborative performance deviser, performer, and teacher. Karen lives and works in London where she has launched Haranczak/Navarre Performance Projects. Her practice includes listening for the unnoticed, the almost invisible, and the very quiet. She was a member of the Chicago-based performance group Goat Island for 20 years until the group disbanded in 2009. With Goat Island, Karen performed and led workshops throughout the USA and the UK, and in Austria, Belgium, Croatia, Germany, Canada and Switzerland. She is an associate artist at Chelsea Theatre (London), and received an honorary fellowship from University College Falmouth.

- www.karenchristopher.co.uk
- @KarenChristoph7

ABIGAIL CONWAY: Subject to_Change

Abigail Conway is a creator of live art performance. Abigail's interests lie in working with material objects and craft to create site-specific installations and immersive experiences for audiences. She is committed to exploring intimacy, within instruction-based works. She is founder, and director, of Subject to_ change, a Live Art Company, which makes small and large-scale, spectator led, installations, to which their show home sweet home has toured to national and international acclaim. The Company is committed to challenging the boundaries of artistic performance. The works of Subject to _change give priority to spectator perception and engagement.

- www.abigailconway.org.uk
- www.subjecttcochange.org.uk
- @abigata

COOL HUNTING: Daniel Hills and Rachel St Clair

Cool Hunting is the collaborative work of Daniel Hills and Rachel St Clair. We are a new performance collaboration formed in early 2013 and based in the South Coast of England. We want to make work which comments on the absurdities of the now and the world we live in. Through task based performance methods in our devising process, we hope to create playful work, which both excites and frustrates our audience. We are committed to making use of the tools at hand and around us and because of this, much of our work is created with a DIY attitude and this same attitude is apparent in our final performances. We are looking to create work that could be performed in a variety of spaces, aside from conventional theatre venues. Over the coming years we hope to play games, make a mess, bare all, tell jokes and have fun, with a few ukulele songs here and there.

- www.coolhuntingtheatre.com
- @TheCoolHunting

RICHARD DEDOMENICI

Richard DeDomenici makes art that is social, playful, critical, political and beautiful - although rarely all at the same time. His low-grade acts of anarcho-surrealist civil disobedience cause the kind of uncertainty that leads to possibility. In 2011 his work was shortlisted for the Arts Foundation Fellowship, nominated for the Jerwood TrustMoving Image Prize, and was an Oxford Samuel Beckett Theatre Trust Award finalist. In 2012 Richard was commissioned to make work at Tate Modern and the National Theatre. He has performed in 23 countries and in 2013 made new work in Thailand, Japan, Belgium, China and Australia.

- www.dedomenici.com
- @DeDomenici

DIRTY MARKET: Jon Lee and Georgina Sowerby

Dirty Market are theatre bricoleurs based in Southeast London. We use open, inventive approaches to make involving performances: group members sometimes swap roles, reflecting our creative ethos. Using bricolage* to make new work, plays are often start-points for pieces and elements are incorporated that tradition would discard. Dirty Market transforms spaces, usually making work in non-theatre buildings as well as in communities where theatre doesn't normally take place. We share our process in supportive, playful workshops that encourage others to generate work too. Our vision is to cultivate an ongoing dialogue with the audience, with our events open to offshoot projects.

- www.dirtymarket.co.uk
- @Dirty_Market

FICTIONAL DOGSHELF: Lee Miller and Joanne 'Bob' Whalley

They travel by night. She worries for him whenever she sees him dancing across the central reservation, silhouetted against the headlights of the oncoming tricks, their air horns a soundtrack to his movements. One nights she

might voice her concerns. That he would be struck by one of these oncoming behemoths, and that she would be left to wander the M6 for all eternity, like some kind of awful wraith. He would smile, take her hand and tell her he could not be harmed. Not of she was always there with the A-Z, to navigate the tricky places and chart what is unchartered. Joanne 'Bob' Whalley and Lee Miller have collaborated on various performance projects since they met in 1992. In 2004 they completed the first joint PhD to be undertaken within a UK Higher Education Institution. Bob is senior Lecturer in Devised Theatre at Dartington College of Art/University College Falmouth and Lee is Programme Manager of the MA Performance Practice at the University of plymouth.

- www.dogshelf.com
- @dogshelf

ANDY FIELD

Andy Field is an artist, writer and curator based in London. He is interested in performances that invite you to reconsider your relationship to the people and places that surround you. His work has been presented in major festivals and venues and in more unexpected spaces, from multi-storey carparks to the Natural History Museum.

- www.andytfield.co.uk
- @andytfield

FOREST FRINGE: Deborah Pearson

Forest Fringe began in 2007 as a totally independent, not-for-profit space in the midst of the Edinburgh Festival. We sought to build a community around this space in which experimentation and adventure were cherished and supported. A space that offered artists and audiences alike a different kind of opportunity – the chance to come together collectively, contributing their time and energy to make exciting, improbable, spectacular things happen. The kind of things that none of us could have achieved individually. In the breathless, unpredictable years since then we've tried to embed these values in everything we've done. We've continued to return to Edinburgh every year, each time looking to experiment with different ways of doing things and new contexts to accommodate even the most unusual experiences. Meanwhile we've also started exploring beyond the festival, creating new collaborative projects up and down the country and year-round events such as our Travelling Sounds Library. In all this we try and serve as a bridge, finding imaginative ways to connect the country's most innovative performance artists and theatremakers with new audiences, new supporters and new contexts for their work. For us Forest Fringe remains an experiment, a creative project that we hope is defined by the same kind of adventurousness and unpredictability that we so love in the artists we work with.

• www.forestfringe.co.uk
• @ForestFringe

GETINTHEBACKOFTHEVAN

GETINTHEBACKOFTHEVAN is a performance company formed in 2008, making cross-genre work that plays with glory, endurance, artifice and the banal. They also curate the work of other artists. GETINTHEBACKOFTHEVAN's work has been shown across London at venues and contexts including Almeida Festival, SPILL Festival, Soho Theatre, The Roundhouse and Battersea Arts Centre, as well as on regular national tours. The company was a Platformed Artist at Arnolfini (Bristol) during 2011, commissioned to respond to the venue's 50th Anniversary theme "The Apparatus of Culture". Internationally, the company's work has been shown at Festival Belluard Bollwerk International (Switzerland), ANTI Festival of Contemporary Art (Finland), PACT Zollverein (Germany), Noorderzon Festival (Netherlands), Junge Hunde Festival (Denmark), Vienna Festwochen and Rote Fabrik (Switzerland). GETINTHEBACKOFTHEVAN is a 2013/14 Artsadmin

Associate Artist and an Associate Company at the Department of Drama, Theatre and Performance at Roehampton University (London).

• www.getinthebackofthevan.com
• @GETINTHEBACK

GOB SQUAD: Sharon Smith

Gob Squad is a group of UK and German artists making mixed media performance, installation and video. We are a collective, the seven core-members work collaboratively on the concept, direction and performance of a work. Also, there is always a close, extended family of other artists, performers and technicians with whom we collaborate. We started the company in Nottingham in 1994. We are now based in Berlin but stay connected to the UK through our research and processes. During the making of a work our process is always very often. Our desire to work with public in a specific and intimate way demands that we 'try out' our ideas/sketches and initial tender structures on friends so that we can see how some kind of interaction feels – for us and for them. 'How' we are communicating is as important as what. The work wants to frame reality. Often site specific, often somehow interactive, it searches for beauty in the everyday. We try to explore the point where theatre meets art, media and real life. Everyday life and magic, banality and utopia, reality and entertainment are all set on a collision course and the audience is often asked to step beyond their traditional role as passive spectators and bear witness to the results. Gob Squad is Johanna Freiburg, Sean Patten, Sharon Smith, Berit Stumpf, Sarah Thom, Bastian Trost and Simon Will.

• www.gobsquad.com

MAMORU IRIGUCHI

Mamoru is a performance maker and theatre designer. The performance works are rooted in his knowledge and experience in theatre design as well as broad interests in 2D and 3D, gender and sexuality, parasitism and symbiosis, fairytales and evolution theories. *Pregnant?!, Into the Skirt , Journey from a Man to a Woman* and *Projector/Conjector* have toured in the UK and internationally. His latest piece is *One Man Show*, commissioned for the Place Prize. His theatre design work includes *Mincemeat* (Cardboard Citizens, Best Design, Evening Standard Theatre Awards) and *The Pink Bits* (Mapping4D, Oxford Samuel Beckett Theatre Award). Mamoru is an Artsadmin associate artist.

- www.iriguchi.co.uk
- @mamoru_iriguchi

BRYONY KIMMINGS

Bryony Kimmings is a Performance Artist based in the East Region. She creates full-length theatre shows, cabaret works, homemade music, sound installations and documentary films. Her work is larger than life, outrageous, visually loud, often dangerous, somewhat unpredictable but above all fun. She is inspired by the taboos and anomalies of British culture and her autobiographical themes promote the airing of her own dirty laundry to oil conversations on seemingly difficult subjects. Her work follows real life social experiments that she embarks upon with genuine genius intrigue and wholehearted, fearless gusto. Bryony's work has been seen in galleries and theatres across the world, most recently at Frieze Art Fair, Soho Theatre, Antifest (Finland), Culturgest (Portugal), Fusebox Festival (Texas), The Southbank Centre, Brighton Festival, Duckie, The Roundhouse, The Barbican, Wales Millennium Centre, Latitude, The Secret Garden Party and Assembly. Her 2010 work *Sex Idiot* won the Total Theatre Award and her 2011 show *7 Day Drunk* was awarded a Brick Award nomination and Time Out Critics Choice award.

- www.bryonykimmings.com
- @BryonyKimmings

LIVE ART DEVELOPMENT AGENCY:
Aaron Wright

The Live Art Development Agency offers Resources, Professional Development Initiatives, Projects and Publishing for the support and development of Live Art practices, and critical discourses in the UK and internationally. The Agency is committed to supporting the high risk artists, practices and ideas of contemporary culture and particularly the practices of emerging artists, and artists from culturally diverse backgrounds. The Agency's four key areas of activity - resources, professional development, projects and publishing - are informed by the guiding principles of working strategically, in partnership, and in consultation. The Live Art Development Agency coordinates Live Art UK, the national network of Live Art promoters.

- www.thisisliveart.co.uk
- @thisisliveart

BRIAN LOBEL

Brian Lobel is a New York-born, London-based performer presenting work in a range of contexts, from medical schools to galleries, cabarets to museums, forests to marketplaces. Performances include *Cruising for Art, Purge, Hold My Hand and We're Halfway There, Carpe Minuta Prima, BALL, Ruach, An Appreciation* and have shown in London, Bangkok, Yokahama, Helsinki, Brussels, Kuopio, Chicago, Austin, San Diego, Paris, Ghent, Santarcangelo, Lisbon, Edinburgh, Manchester and beyond. Brian is a Senior Lecturer at University of Chichester in Performing Arts, a Core Member of Forest Fringe, and an Associate Artist with Clod Ensemble's Performing Medicine.

- www.blobelwarming.com
- @blobelwarming

LOW PROFILE: Hannah Jones and Rachel Dobbs

LOW PROFILE is a collaboration between artists Rachel Dobbs (IRL) and Hannah Jones (UK) working together to make live art since 2003. They are currently based in Plymouth and Penzance. LOW PROFILE's work is about not giving up, the impossible, the endless and the obsessive, our experiences of everyday life magnified and put on show. Over the last number of years, their research and work has been concerned with the timely and persistent themes of survival and preparedness, alongside the perceived need for protection from others, the unknown and ourselves. Recently, LOW PROFILE have been making a series of works under the umbrella name *DRY RUN*, exploring simulations of situations often yet to be experienced, pre-planned dress rehearsals, stand-ins and practice runs for the 'real thing'. By setting up situations that are inviting and engaging, they explore the reoccurring concerns of being prepared, trying hard and doing your best, learning live and making mistakes. The work takes various shapes including live performance, video, installation, artists' ephemera, publications and bookworks.

• www.we-are-low-profile.co.uk
• @LP_LOWPROFILE

MADE IN CHINA: Jess Latowicki and Tim Cowbury

Made In China is the collaborative work of Tim Cowbury and Jessica Latowicki. We make visceral shows at the juncture of playwriting and live art, for audiences who are fans of neither and both. So far, the shows have been physical, playful, excessive and destructive. We are drawn to great stories but like to disrupt them with things like bad dancing, beer downing, interval training and downright lying. Each show makes its own rules. And each show aims to ask the audience difficult questions whilst giving them a really good time. Made In China formed in 2009. We have performed our work across the UK and

beyond, at venues including: The National Theatre, The ICA, The Junction, Warwick Arts Centre, Hull Truck Theatre, Tobacco Factory Theatre, BAC, Arcola Theatre, Forest Fringe, La MaMa ETC (New York), InTacto Festival (Vitoria Spain) and The Paradiso (Amsterdam). Made In China were a National Theatre Studio Affiliate Company from 2010-2012. Our show Gym Party was nominated for an Arches Brick Award in 2013.

• www.madeinchinatheatre.com
• @MadeInChinaThtr

MILK PRESENTS: Lucy Doherty, Adam Robertson and Ruby Glaskin

Milk Presents are Lucy Doherty, Adam Robertson and Ruby Glaskin. They make low-fi devised performance that explores and critiques the representation of gender and sexuality in stories and popular culture. Their work is messy, lyrical and visually striking. Hand drawn acetates animate scenes on overhead projectors, bikes are pedalled by performers to generate power and Heath Robinson contraptions manipulate set. The company are based in the UK, and tour their work across the country as well as internationally.

• www.milkpresents.com
• @MilkPresents

HANNAH NICKLIN

Hannah Nicklin is a post-doc, producer and practising artist working in the areas of game design, agency, interactive theatre, and art-and-play-as-activism.
After completing a PhD in the political power of first person theatre in the digital age at Loughborough University, Hannah joined Hide&Seek - a game design studio - as a research associate - she also does research for UWE, and talks and teaches in industry and academic settings on digital technology, activism, and DIY/Punk theatre. Her own practice in theatre, installation and game

design is often based in community work or storytelling, and almost always happens outside of traditional arts venues. She produced Performance in the Pub 'pay what you can nights out for people who don't really 'do' theatre' in Leicester for over a year, bringing DIY experimental performance to a gig space and gig-going people, and is involved in producing a new mobile web app with albow.com which allows people to share, discover and exchange value in disruptive ways around live events.

- www.hannahnicklin.com
- @hannahnicklin

MICHAEL PINCHBECK

Michael Pinchbeck is a writer, live artist and theatre maker based in Nottingham (UK). He co-founded Metro-Boulot-Dodo in 1997 after studying Theatre and Creative Writing at Lancaster University. He left the company in 2004 to embark on a five-year live art project – *The Long and Winding Road*, performed at the ICA (London), Ikon Gallery (Birmingham) and The Bluecoat (Liverpool). He was commissioned by Nottingham Playhouse to write *The White Album* (2006) and *The Ashes* (2011) and was recently awarded funding from the British Council to research and develop a new theatre project – *Bolero*. Michael is currently working on a trilogy of devised performances inspired by Shakespeare plays: *The Beginning*, *The Middle* and *The End*. In 2012, he was a creative ambassador for World Event Young Artists in Nottingham. His work has been selected three times for the British Council's Edinburgh Showcase. He has a Masters in Performance and Live Art from Nottingham Trent University and is undertaking a PhD at Loughborough University exploring the role of the dramaturg. Michael is a co-director of Hatch, a live art platform in the East Midlands, and lectures at the University of Lincoln.

- www.michaelpinchbeck.co.uk
- @mdpinchbeck

RESIDENCE: Ella Good and Nicki Kent

Residence is a collective of 17 artists, we share space, resources, knowledge and opportunities. We make live performance, including live art, script based work, devised performance, community and interactive work, we are united by a curiosity towards each others practices, and a commitment to supporting each other. Our work takes us all over the world, look at the blog and our members page to see what we are all up to. We currently reside in the milk bar, a tall and thin Victorian shop in the centre of Bristol inside which we make things happen; new work, workshops, eating, drinking, occasionally sleeping, thinking, yoga, we have tiny ideas, make new and old collaborations, and other things too.

- www.residence.org.uk
- @residence1

SEARCH PARTY: Pete Phillips and Jodie Hawkes

'...unique storytelling that feels absolutely of the place.'
The Guardian (UK)

Search Party is the collaboration of artists Jodie Hawkes and Pete Phillips. Since 2005 Search Party have created performances for theatres and public spaces throughout the UK and internationally. Search Party's work has playfully explored ideas of sport, ageing and the relationship between people and places. They are committed to making immediate, hopeful performances that engage diverse audiences. Search Party's work attempts to re-negotiate the relationship between artist and audience, creating temporary communities, inviting spectators to become co-collaborators in the live event. Search Party are members of Residence, an artist-led organisation based in Bristol, comprising of artists and companies who make theatre, performance and live art.

- www.searchpartyperformance.org.uk
- @search_party

SLEEPING TREES: Josh George Smith, James Dunnell Smith and John Woodburn

Sleeping Trees is James Dunnell-Smith, Joshua George Smith and John Woodburn: a trio of award winning, multi-medium storytellers. Their work is rooted in comedy, mime and live performance, and uses stories and established texts as starting points of departure and improvisation. The company have completed a trilogy project titled, 'The Stories Project'; the re-creation of stories without the use of props, scenery or costume, encouraging their audience to use their imaginations when engaging with the work, just as they would if they were reading a book. The stories focused on are those with particular significance to the artist's childhoods and are devised from memory alone. Any detail the company cannot remember is susceptible to the eccentric, often inaccurate creativity of the trio in order to complete the story. The first story to get the Sleeping Trees treatment was Enid Blyton's *Magic Faraway Tree*, which made its debut at the 2010 Edinburgh Fringe Festival. The company were then nominated for a Total Theatre Award for the following show: *Not Treasure Island*. The final instalment; *The Sleeping Trees Odyssey*, became the FMN Editors Choice as the winners of the Fringe 'ones to watch' award 2013.

- www.sleepingtreestheatre.co.uk
- @WeSleepingTrees

SHATTER RESISTANT: Eleanor Massie and Sophie Rose

Friends since the age of eight, in 2012 we formed as a company. Our debut show is *Cathy's Kitchen*. Portable and low-fi, it uses comedy to interrogate questions of autobiography, contemporary culture, death and gender identity. We both have solo projects and work day jobs. Sophie juggles the books as Company Manager for Gandini Juggling. Eleanor reads some books for an AHRC funded doctoral research project at Queen Mary University.

- www.fragilerules.wordpress.com
- @FRAGILE_RULES

SLEEPDOGS: Tanuja Amarasuriya & Timothy X Atack

Sleepdogs is a collaboration between writer/composer Timothy X Atack and director/producer Tanuja Amarasuriya. We work with stories and prompts to the imagination using theatre, film, sound and whatever else feels right. We're interested in hybrid genres, the splicing of traditions, mixing and matching. As collaborators, we share a love of finding common ground in seemingly conflicting material and believe it's the in-between spaces where you find the truly interesting stuff: stories that haven't been told quite that way before, scenic routes not yet taken, familiar emotions made complex again. Our work has been commissioned and presented by Bristol Old Vic, Forest Fringe, Paines Plough, Seattle International Film Festival, BBC Radio and others. Tim also plays with the band, Angel Tech, and is an artist in residence at Pervasive Media Studio, Watershed. Tanuja also works for Theatre Bristol and has worked as a dramaturg and/or director with Sam Halmarack, Raucous Collective and Tobacco Factory Theatre. We are based in Bristol, UK

- www.sleepdogs.org
- @sleepdogs

SLEEPWALK COLLECTIVE: Sammy Metcalfe

Sleepwalk Collective is an award-winning live-art and experimental theatre group creating fragile, nocturnal performances between the UK and Spain. Formed in London in 2006 by Iara Solano Arana (Spain), Malla Sofia Pessi (Finland) and Sammy Metcalfe (UK), and based from 2007-13 in Vitoria-Gasteiz in the Spanish Basque Country, the company currently lives and works in Madrid. Shows include *As The Flames Rose We Danced To The Sirens*, *The Sirens* (premiered 2010), *Amusements* (2012), and *Karaoke* (2013).

- www.sleepwalkcollective.com
- @Sleepw_lk

STANS CAFE: James Yarker
Stan's Cafe is a group of artists from a variety of disciplines, though primarily theatre practitioners, working under the artistic direction of James Yarker. The company consists of a core of long term collaborators and a range of associated artists. The line up changes according to the project being worked upon. Graeme and James agreed to form the company whilst eating at Stan's Cafe, just off Brick Lane in London. We wanted an unusual name, but one that wasn't too aggressive, too posturing, a cheap joke, a bad pun or overly earnest. Station House Opera had always seemed a good name, mainly because they didn't do opera. So there you go... Oh yes and it's pronounced Caff.
- www.stanscafe.co.uk
- @stanscafe

STOKE NEWINGTON INTERNATIONAL AIRPORT: Gary Campbell
Gary Campbell is a Freelance Designer-Deviser-Makerist and an Associate Lecturer on the FAD and BA Performance design and practice courses at Central St Martins, UAL. He is Co-Artistic Director of Stoke Newington International Airport and makes work with his partner Jeannine Inglis Hall. His practice is varied and ever changing but generally involves designing social spaces for performance, drinking and living. Within these spaces he creates dynamic events that encourage the experimentation and interaction of both artist and audience.
- www.stkinternational.co.uk
- www.pandorastreet.blogspot.co.uk
- @STK_Int

STOKE NEWINGTON INTERNATIONAL AIRPORT: Greg McLaren
Greg McLaren is an artist operating in all realms of performance, from opera to interactive, performance art to plays. He makes unusual, exciting and provocative work for audiences which attempts to transform witnesses into an active audience as 'popular incitement to self-action and environmental transformation' (Jeffrey Shaw, concepts for an operative art, 1969). His interest is in the moment of encounter - where the performance lies, where status and identity are established. He founded Stoke Newington International Airport in 2008 and since then his work has been performed at and supported by BAC, MAC Birmingham, Cambridge Junction, National Portrait Gallery, Soho Theatre, Science Museum and in several countries beyond. He is a British Council Young Creative Entrepreneur.
- www.stkinternational.co.uk
- www.gregmclaren.com
- @Zanzibarbeer

THE SUITCASE ROYALE: Joseph O'Farrell
Joseph O'Farrell (JOF) is a multi-art performer, producer, curator, musician and lecturer from Melbourne, Australia. He is a founding member of Junkyard theatre company, The Suitcase Royale; a trio that has been touring new Australian theatre works nationally and internationally since 2004. The Suitcase Royale coined the term Junkyard Theatre to describe their work. A seemless combination of live music, live operation and image-based theatre which is largely constructed from second hand materials and junk. The term is now broadly used in Australia to describe theatre work with this ethos. Joseph's continues to explore these principles in his solo practice and has extended it to community and artist led events. His ability to work across genres has also allowed him to inspire young and emerging performance makers around the globe as a lecturer and workshop leader.
- www.thesuitcaseroyale.com
- www.jofmakesart.com
- @SuitcaseRoyale

THEATRE BRISTOL: Tanuja Amarasuriya

Theatre Bristol is a collective of producers whose role is to work with artists, producers, venues and others to enable the best live performance to be made and experienced in Bristol. Theatre Bristol's central ethos is that when you share stuff, everyone gets better; and our activity focuses on sharing good information, culturing strong networks, being open, offering bespoke artist and producer support and development, encouraging independent and alternative thinking, and testing out new models of working that can help artists make inspiring, transformative art for the world. Tanuja Amarasuriya is a theatre director and producer. She is Co-Executive Producer of Theatre Bristol and Co-Artistic Director of Sleepdogs.

• www.theatrebristol.net/about
• @theatrebristol

THIRD ANGEL: Alexander Kelly

Third Angel makes entertaining and original contemporary performance that speaks directly, honestly and engagingly to its audience. Established in Sheffield in 1995, the company makes work that encompasses performance, theatre, live art, installation, film, video art, documentary, photography and design. We use styles, techniques and interests discovered in our more experimental work for other spaces, to create new theatre that plays with conventional forms while remaining accessible to a mainstream audience. Third Angel has shown work in theatres, galleries, cinemas, office blocks, car parks, swimming baths, on the internet and TV, in school halls, a damp cellar in Leicester and a public toilet in Bristol. The company has shown work at festivals and venues across the UK and mainland Europe, including Germany, Hungary, Switzerland, Belgium, Portugal, France and Spain. Third Angel's artistic work is supported and invigorated by an active Creative Learning programme that includes practical projects with students and other artists, project supervision, mentoring, lecturing, after-show talks and discussions.

• www.thirdangel.co.uk
• @thirdangeluk

CHRIS THORPE

Chris Thorpe was a founder member of Unlimited Theatre and still works and tours with the company. He is also an Artistic Associate of live art/theatre company Third Angel as well as working closely with, among others, Forest Fringe, Slung Low, Chris Goode, RashDash, Belarus Free Theatre and Portuguese company mala voadora for whom he has just completed a trilogy of new plays. He has an ongoing collaboration with poet Hannah Jane Walker, and their shows *The Oh Fuck Moment* and *I Wish I Was Lonely* are published by Oberon Books. As a playwright Chris has written radio and stage drama, as well as translating the work of Ugljesa Sajtinac (the play *Huddersfield* is also published by Oberon), Belarus Free Theatre, and Ze Maria Mendes. He also writes and performs solo work, plays guitar in the political noise/performance project #TORYCORE and works as a selector for the National Student Drama Festival.

• @piglungs

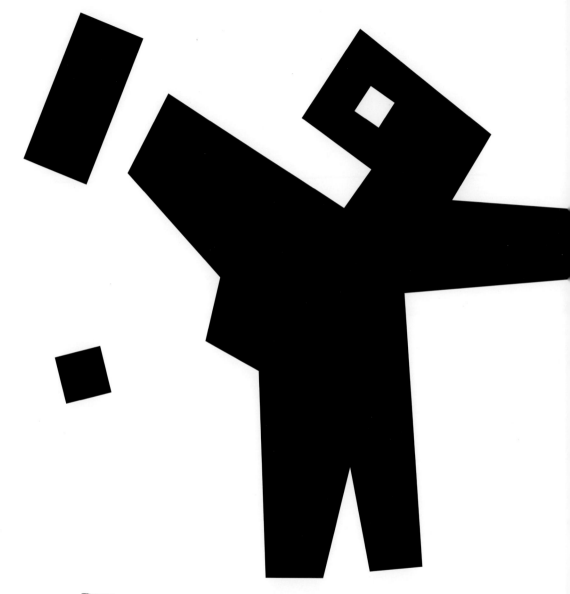

Acknowledgements

Gushing "thank you's", and dignified hat-tipping to special people...

Handshakes, and research-related knowing nods for my colleagues and friends at the University of Chichester, especially: Chris Anderson, Jane Bacon, Andy Dixon, Graham Roy Donaldson, Ben Francombe, Donna Kirstein, Julie Peachy, Anthony Walsh and Emma White. Goes to show that i did NOT "do it myself". An over-enthusiatic chest-five goes to James Baker, for casting a positive critical eye over my own contribution to this book, as well as secret handshakes to Becki Haines and Andy Roberts — the 'rest' of Bootworks — for supporting me in this little journey. Lois Keiden and Aaron Wright at LADA have been a great help from the start of this project: giving me advice and support as i navigated my way haphazardly through curating, making and getting this book out there: all of which i knew absolutely nothing about before i started.

Thanks most of all to the artists, collectives and organisations that have supported this project and contributed. Without them this book would be substantially smaller, and obviously less impressive.

And to Jesus. Everyone thanks him (or someone like him) these days don't they? He didn't write anything for this book, but apparently — even though I'm agnostic — i'll go to hell if i don't thank him. I think that's a bit much. it's just a book. But i'll be that guy repenting on his death bed one day, 'just in case', and so i better give the ol' JC a knowing wink at least.

Disclaimer

The opinions expressed by the contributors and the main author are theirs alone, and do not reflect the opinions of the University of Chichester or any employee thereof. The university and main author are not responsible for the accuracy of any of the information supplied by the contributors.